VINCE LOMBARDI

MEMORIES OF A SPECIAL TIME

VINCE LOMBARDI

MEMORIES OF A SPECIAL TIME

Edited
by
MIKE BYNUM

𝔒𝔠𝔱𝔬𝔟𝔢𝔯 𝔍𝔬𝔬𝔱𝔟𝔞𝔩𝔩 𝔆𝔬𝔯𝔭.

Portions of this book have been previously published. Listed below is their original source of publication:

Chapters 1-18 first appeared in a series of newspaper articles written by Robert W. Wells in *The Milwaukee Journal* from September 27, 1970 to October 18, 1970.

Chapter 19 first appeared in the January 1962 issue of *Sport* magazine.

Chapter 20 first appeared in the September 5, 1967 issue of *Look* magazine.

Chapter 21 first appeared in the September 19, 1967 issue of *Look* magazine.

Chapter 22 first appeared in the September 27, 1968 issue of *Life* magazine. Reprinted by permission of Time-Life, Inc.

Chapter 23 first appeared in the August 1969 issue of *The Washingtonian.* Reprinted by permission of Washington Magazine, Inc.

Chapter 24 first appeared in the September 1970 issue of *The Washingtonian.* Reprinted by permission of Washington Magazine, Inc.

Chapter 25 first appeared in the 1966 publication of *Championship: The Complete N.F.L. Title Story.* Reprinted by permission of Jerry Izenberg.

Chapter 26 first appeared in the 1970 publication *Lombardi: The Man, the Coach, the Legend.* Reprinted by permission of Jerry Izenberg.

Afterword first appeared in the 1973 publication of *Vince Lombardi on Football.* Reprinted by permission of Wallynn, Inc.

Jacket Cover Artwork: Dennis Luzak, Greenwich, CT
Jacket Cover Design: David Hirsch Design Group, Chicago, IL
Book Design: O'Rourke Graphics, Chicago, IL
Book Lithograph: R.R. Donnelley & Sons Company, Chicago, IL

ISBN: 0-945718-02-0
Library of Congress Catalog Card Number: 88-62021

To Pina Marie,
A questa personal molta speciale che mi ha inspirare di divenire fare il mio propio meglio. Ciao con amore!
Michael

Contents

VINCE LOMBARDI

MEMORIES OF A SPECIAL TIME

Foreword

His was a time for greatness and for glory.

In 10 very memorable seasons, Vince Lombardi dominated professional football. Beginning in 1959, in his first season as head coach, he took the worst team in the National Football League, the Green Bay Packers, and turned them into winners. In the eight seasons that followed they won six divisional titles, five N.F.L. championships and the first two Super Bowls. Then in 1969, after one restless season away from coaching, Lombardi began to use the same magic again on the Washington Redskins and promptly drove them to their first winning season in 14 years. It was, indeed, a very special time.

Unfortunately, on September 3, 1970, at the beginning of the time of the year which he loved best, Fate intervened. Stricken at the age of 57 by intestinal cancer, one of our greatest heroes was suddenly gone.

Vince Lombardi: Memories of a Special Time is a colleciton of the greatest stories ever written about the Coach. They were penned by some of the best sportswriters in the country — W.C. Heinz, Joe Donnelly, Robert W. Wells, Jerry Izenberg and Tom Dowling. Together, their stories on Lombardi have weaved a master portrait of an individual who All-Pro Packer guard and noted author Jerry Kramer once called " a cruel, kind, tough, gentle, miserable, wonderful man whom I often hate and often love and always respect."

Loved, hated, admired, feared, praised and condemned — a man who aroused only the strongest of emotions — Lombardi pushed, kicked and led his teams to the top of the professional football world. In the process they were to forever change the cultural lifestyle and thinking habits of the American public.

Vince Lombardi: Memories of a Special Time is the inspiring story of professional football's greatest coach, his winning football men and the dynasty that they built together. Here you will follow Lombardi from the early, formative years where he labored in obscurity at Fordham, St. Cecilia High School and West Point, then later as an assistant to Jim Lee Howell with the New York Giants, and finally those unforgettable years with the Packers and the Redskins. Here are the battles that he and his teams endured together: the championships won, the miracles, the glory, the tears. Most importantly, you'll learn of the real impact that Lombardi, the coach, had upon his men as he drove them to obtain a pinnacle of success that has never again been equaled by any team, in any sport.

This moving biography is a serious and in-depth attempt into the true character of Lombardi, the individual, and the great legacy that he left behind. Pro football greats like Paul Hornung, Jim Taylor, Bart Starr, Ray Nitschke, Frank Gifford, Charley Conerly, Sonny Jurgensen and many other lesser knowns have allowed their memories and their experiences with one another, and with Lombardi, to be brought together to describe this special time in their lives.

Vince Lombardi: Memories of a Special Time is a story about courage and commitment. Most importantly, it is a story about winning and what it does to all of us.

Mike Bynum
Birmingham, Alabama
July 8, 1988

BOOK I

Do you not know that in a race all the runners compete, but only one receives the prize? So run that you may obtain it.

I Corinthians 9:24

Vince Lombardi: The Biography of a Legend

1

When Vince's Era Began

Professional football's Lombardi Era began with seven minutes left to play in the first Packers' game of the 1959 season.

Until that moment on a rainy Sept. 27, only the most optimistic Green Bay backer imagined that the arrival of a former New York Giants assistant coach to take charge would be worth more than a line of type in the history of the game.

True, the team had won four of six exhibition games — three more victories than in its last regular season. But such games don't count. Now Green Bay was playing the Chicago Bears in the 1959 opener and it was losing.

Its offensive team seemed no better than the one that had cost Coach Ray "Scooter" McLean his job the year before. The fans took some comfort from the Packers' defense, however.

It had held the Bears to a 46-yard field goal in the first half and another three points early in the fourth quarter. But the way things were going with the offense, Chicago's 6-0 lead looked big enough.

There were 32,150 spectators in City Stadium in Green Bay — a capacity crowd for a change. Some of them were getting their first glimpse of Vincent T. Lombardi, standing near the sidelines in a rumpled tan raincoat.

He had added poundage since his college days, when he had been a 175-pound lineman, but he was only 5 feet 9 inches tall. In their helmets and shoulder pads, his players loomed over this stocky fellow with the Brooklyn accent who exulted openly when a play went well and cried out in anger or despair with it failed.

It was no secret in Green Bay that the new man had descended on the squad like a combination of Capt. Bligh, Savonarola and Emperor Caesar Augustus.

Very little that happened to the Packers was a secret at such fan headquarters as Martha's Cafe or Holzer's Drugstore. The consensus before the season started was that Lombardi was the tough taskmaster needed to snap the Pack out of its losing habits, its 1-10-1 record of '58, and the humiliation of being nicknamed a conga team because it kept going one, two, three, kick.

But except for the obvious improvement in the defense, there wasn't much excuse for cheering that afternoon 11 years ago in the first 53 minutes of the game.

Lamar McHan gained 101 yards passing. But in Bear territory, it seemed, he either missed his target or the ball bounced out of the receiver's hand. The former Chicago Cardinal quarterback had been obtained to give the team a new leader, so even after he began to limp from a muscle pull in the second quarter, Lombardi kept him in the game. Bart Starr was on the bench. In 1959, even an injured McHan was considered his superior.

A rugged second-year man from Louisiana State, Jim Taylor, was considered a pretty fair ballcarrier, but the other running back, Paul Hornung, had shown little since he arrived from Notre Dame. The coaches had never been sure whether the college star was a halfback, fullback or quarterback.

Hornung had shared the doubt until the new coach gave him the word. He was his halfback, Lombardi informed him, and the only way Paul could get out of the job was to get killed.

Between them, Hornung and Taylor carried the ball 41 times that afternoon, but whenever the Packers started to move, someone fumbled, someone was penalized or one of those passes by McHan slipped away. Often it was necessary to punt the ball to the Bears and it was time for the defensive team to struggle some more.

Now it was the final period, the time when conditioning pays dividends. Arms and shoulders ache by then, leg muscles move more sluggishly, the bruises hurt, the mind is less alert. Everyone is affected but the man who is in shape is affected less.

Whatever its shortcomings, this Packer team of 1959 was certainly in shape. The conditioning process its members had gone through before the season began was like nothing the players had experienced before.

The fine for being overweight was $10 a day — the same charge was made for skipping one of the three daily meals — but that was only money. A worse penalty was the Lombardi tongue — "Mister, you run like a cow," he would yell, tailoring his Brooklyn invective to this bucolic setting. Worst of all was the necessity to keep going through grass drills and wind sprints when every muscle demanded rest.

The grass drills consisted of running in one place, flopping down, leaping up and running again, repeating the process interminably until Lombardi was satisfied. The wind sprints required everyone to run full speed for 30 or 40 yards, then back, again, until Lombardi was satisfied.

"No one was permitted to dog it," according to the testimony of Phil Bengtson, who had come from the San Francisco 49ers to coach the defensive team. "Soon almost all were able to survive. Nobody vomited after the first couple of days."

Bengtson's defensive squad lost an average of 12 pounds per man during the first six weeks of training — one member, Dave "Hawg" Hanner, dropped 20. When Lombardi was out of earshot, there was groaning and griping.

But after surviving his conditioning program the men believed they could survive anything, including the end of the world, and here it was the fourth quarter and the Bears were still not able to approach the Packers' goal.

With eight of the final 15 minutes gone, Max McGee punted from Green Bay's 29 to the Bear 17. A Chicago rookie fumbled the runback on the 26. Jim Ringo, the Packers' center, recovered.

Lombardi was on his feet, pounding his fist against his hand. McHan went limping out with the offensive team for what might be the Packers' last chance to score in the new coach's first regular season game.

Not even those 11 players remember now exactly what went through their brains then, but it seems likely that a single thought crossed several minds: If they came off the field again without a touchdown, the coach would not be pleased.

For reasons often debated, Lombardi aroused mingled feelings of fear, pride and fierce loyalty in his muscular troops.

He had ended his halftime exhortation by shouting, "Go through that door and bring back victory." Linebacker Bill Forester leaped up with the others and cracked his arm against a locker, the most painful injury he was to receive all year.

"Now it's time to score, and to win," Lombardi had also told them at halftime. Time was running out. They had not scored. The order hung over their helmets like a thunderhead.

In weeks of practice, Lombardi had stressed the basics — blocking and tackling, with the ballcarrier looking for a momentary chink in the opponents' living wall and plunging through it. So now McHan handed off to Hornung, who gained a few difficult yards, and then to Taylor, who got his kicks from knocking an opponent sprawling.

The Bears stopped Hornung, but not until he had made a first down and then, on the fifth play after Ringo clutched the fumble, it was Taylor's turn again and he was five yards away from a score.

Five yards is a long distance on the ground that close to the goal line. The Bears were famous for their defense. But the Chicagoans had not gone through the kind of grass drills and wind sprints that had seemed a few weeks before to be beyond human endurance. They had not survived that degree of organized torture which was to become a Lombardi trademark.

McHan called a play which was not yet known as the Green Bay Sweep — it was, in fact, a play the Giants had often used while Lombardi was New York's offensive coach. As Taylor followed his blockers around right end and scored, the crowd got a preview of its effectiveness.

Hornung had missed field goals from the 19- and the 14-yard lines, but he kicked the point-after-touchdown which made it 7-6. That was margin enough, although in the last minute of play, Hanner tackled Chicago's quarterback, Ed Brown, in the Bears' end zone for a safety, so the final score read 9-6.

Lew Carpenter was closest to Lombardi when the game ended. He grabbed him. As other players converged on them, Lew tried to lift him to his shoulder. The Packers were inexperienced at victory celebrations — they got used to them later — and Carpenter and his helpers nearly fumbled the coach.

But after some cheerful confusion, Lombardi rode jubilantly toward the dressing room on his players' shoulders while the fans yelled and pounded each other on the back and prepared for the biggest impromptu celebration Green Bay had seen in years.

Beating the Bears is always worth a celebration there, but this was something more than that. Before Lombardi's arrival, the Packers had not only been the worst team in the league, but the perennial question of whether Green Bay could continue to compete with cities 10 to 100 times its size had been raised once more.

Lombardi had kept saying he was no miracle man. But he had also said he had not come to lose. As the excitement of his league debut faded, those who had seen the game remembered the fumbles, the missed passes, the mistakes, but mostly they remembered the final score.

"Winning isn't everything," Lombardi was to say often, after the time came that his words were respectfully noted down as philosophical pears. "It's the only thing."

The quotation was not yet part of the legend that grew up around this complicated man. But as they filed happily out of City Stadium just 11 years ago, the fans didn't need to be told that those figures on the scoreboard were what counted, that the lean days were over and that a new football era had begun.

2

The Early Days

Even to most residents of the four other boroughs of New York City, Brooklyn is unknown turf. Few strangers go there except from unavoidable necessity. From the west bank of the East River, Brooklyn is viewed as a great, gray warren filled with inhabitants who speak a special tongue and, when Vince Lombardi lived there, cheered for a team whose designation came from an outdated nickname.

Residents on the Long Island side of the Brooklyn Bridge were once known derisively as Trolley Dodgers, which is how the ballplayers who performed in the raffish intimacy of Ebbets Field got their title. Amusement was the sentiment often aroused by this team and condescending hilarity was the usual reaction of non-Brooklynites to the entire community.

Mention of the borough was a sure laugh in a vaudeville comedian's routine, although Brooklyn — or Breuckelen, as the Dutch spelled it — was a flourishing community when much of Manhattan was used only to pasture cows.

Until its marriage to New York City in 1898, Brooklyn was a separate city, and if the union had not been consummated it would still be larger than Philadelphia. No matter what outlanders think, its 71 square miles are not filled with identical dingy buildings.

As in any other community, there are good neighborhoods and bad. When Vincent was born to Harry and Matilda Lombardi on

June 11, 1913, the family lived in a two-story house in one of the more attractive sections, Sheepshead Bay. His aunt now lives in that building and his parents remain only a few doors away.

More than half a century later, when Vince Lombardi's word was considered gospel on many subjects, he was holding his regular Five O'clock Club on the balcony of a Florida motel suite. He studied the wind and remarked that a northeast wind means three days of bad weather.

"Coach, you know everything," someone said, and the remark was not tinged with sarcasm, for Lombardi's team was picked to win its second straight Super Bowl that winter.

"When you're brought up on the ocean, you get to know such things," the Packers' unchallenged leader explained. Then, still making conversation, he turned to a newcomer. "You live on the ocean?"

"No," the Manhattanite said, not thinking. "I live in New York."

Lombardi's piano key smile widened. It reminded the victim of his last visit to the feline house in the Bronx Zoo.

"Where do you think New York is?" Vince demanded. "New York's right on the ocean. Everybody knows New York's right on the ocean.

But the truth is that most of Manhattan's canyon dwellers do not know this, unless they look at a map. They do not think of themselves as living on the Atlantic, although they do, because to see the open ocean it is necessary to go to some place like Jones Island and look at it.

If you live in the part of New York City called Sheepshead Bay, however, you know you're on the seacoast which indicates that Lombardi was still thinking of the world in terms of Brooklyn even during those years when he could get a table at Toots Shor's without a reservation.

Vincent was the oldest of the five children born to the Lombardis over a 17-year period. He has been called the son of an Italian immigrant and that is technically correct, although Harry Lombardi arrived in the United States when he was too young to remember much about Italy.

Harry's father was a silk merchant who migrated with his family to the United States in the expectation of continuing to deal in silk. This plan didn't work out so Vincent's grandfather went into the trucking business — horses and wagons at first, then trucks.

As the grandfather's sons grew up they helped out, so Harry Lombardi was in the trucking business as a young man. Then he became a wholesale butcher, leaving home early to haul meat to Washington Market near the Hudson, dickering with buyers from stores and restaurants.

Following the family pattern established by the silk merchant, Vincent's father introduced his sons to the virtues of work as soon as they were old enough. This was the custom in the old fishing port called Sheepshead Bay, which was occupied mostly by families who were seeking a firmer toehold in a land to which they or their parents had migrated.

Harry Lombardi's wife had been one of 13 children born to a Sheepshead Bay family named Izzo, so the Lombardi children had a plentiful supply of aunts and uncles, cousins and nieces and nephews.

No one had yet suggested that Vincent was a miracle worker in those boyhood days in Brooklyn, but Mrs. Lombardi's ability to feed a multitude was regarded by her children as close to supernatural.

It didn't seem to matter to her if an extra dozen guests showed up at a table set for the Lombardis. Vince might bring home Joe Goettischeim, who lived a block away from the house on E. 14th St., or a cousin or two. When they were old enough, Harold and Joseph, the two other boys, felt free to invite anyone and the girls, Madeline and Claire, brought home friends.

Assorted relatives often managed to be in the vicinity when the aroma of boiling pasta was wafted on the salt air of Sheepshead Bay, a priest or two might drop around and Matilda Lombardi could never be sure 10 minutes before meal time whether she'd be serving 7 or 12 or 20. But somehow there was always plenty to go around.

When they grew up, her children remembered Mrs. Lombardi as a warm, understanding woman, the family peacemaker, the one who thought things out instead of acting from impulse. Their father, on the other hand, was a stern disciplinarian who brooked no back talk.

The oldest Lombardi son turned out to be a complicated kind of man — dictatorial, impatient, driving, demanding, ambitious, with a volatile temper, but sometimes surprisingly sentimental, warm and sensitive, a man who was both hated and loved. The diverse personalities of his parents provide a partial explanation of the interesting mixture of Lombardi's character.

Vince worked with his father as a boy, using a knife or cleaver on the beef carcasses, carrying loads of meat, learning that the way to earn respect was to work hard, do a job right and not complain.

"Hurt is in the mind," Harry Lombardi once said to Vince, and many years later, when the son had his first head-coaching job in professional football, he still remembered.

On the second day after he took charge in Green Bay, Lombardi found a dozen young men awaiting treatment in the trainer's room.

"What's this?" he shouted. "You've got to play with those small hurts, you know."

Any player who could walk left quickly. From that moment it was understood that anything less than a broken leg was no excuse. The voice in the trainer's room was Vince's, but the Spartan philosophy was imported from Sheepshead Bay.

When a reception was held for Lombardi after he moved to Washington to coach the Redskins, Rene Carpenter, the former wife of astronaut Scott Carpenter, watched him come into the room.

"All of a sudden," she said later, "my skirt was too short and my back was too bare. We were reduced to feeling like children."

"You were afraid to do something wrong in front of him," a man who knew the coach intimately said recently. This was a common reaction to a man who made a career of insisting that any effort less than 100% — some said 110% — was not enough.

"He tolerates perfection," it was said of Vince Lombardi, "provided it is real good."

The same remark could have been made about Harry Lombardi, the meat wholesaler, if the memories of those who knew him in their youth can be trusted. The coach's insistence that there were two ways to do things — the Lombardi way and the wrong way — also owed a debt to parental guidance.

When Vince Lombardi became famous, some tried to fit him into the traditional pattern of the poor boy who made good. Actually, however, the Lombardis were not poor. They lived in a pleasant house in a decent neighborhood. There was money for necessities and minor luxuries. Everyone worked hard, but that was no hardship.

"Anything could turn into a party," someone who remembered the old days at Sheepshead Bay recalled. Whatever the cause of

Vince's driving ambition may have been, it was apparently not an unhappy childhood.

If there was rebellion against the strict home discipline, it was short-lived. When he was grown, Lombardi still regarded his father with admiration.

"He was a perfectionist," he said once, meaning the description as a compliment, "a perfectionist if there ever was one."

There was the time when the elder Lombardi decided to renovate the basement under the gray frame house on E. 14th St. and to tear down a barn that was no longer needed in the back yard, now that horses were out of date.

Vince was old enough to have ideas of his own about how the job should be done. But the way it was done was Harry Lombardi's way, with ready criticism for imperfections and praise for doing it right. When the new concrete floor had hardened and the job was finished, the boy was paid — there were no allowances in the Lombardi family. Money was earned.

When he was 12, Vince was an altar boy at St. Mark's Church. Joe Goettischeim was also an altar boy. They became friends.

The boys went to the movies often — Vince liked movies — and although Joe was only mildly interested in football they saw a lot of games. The Lombardi boy was mild mannered most of the time. With strangers, he seemed shy. But if you were his friend, Joe discovered, you usually did what he wanted to do.

Sometimes they went to the Polo Grounds, which was not close to Sheepshead Bay. Once they got on the subway and made the long ride because Vince wanted to see Bo Molenda play pro football.

A lot of Sheepshead Bay boys had never heard of Bo Molenda, but Lombardi knew all about him, and so he and Joe Goettischeim rode from deep in Brooklyn to the Polo Grounds because that's what Vince wanted to do.

3

A Block of Granite

On an evening in 1936, Father Harold Mulqueen had been relaxing with fellow priests at the Jesuit residence on the Fordham University campus on Rose Hill in the Bronx. Shortly after 11 p.m., he strolled back to St. John's Hall, where about half of the school's 250 boarding students lived.

Father Mulqueen was prefect of the dormitory, so he was charged with enforcing rules that 1970's crop of students would find hard to believe. There was a compulsory study period in the form from 7:30 to 10 p.m. Mondays through Thursdays. On Fridays, a college boy could stay out until 10 and even on Saturday only until 11 p.m. without special permission.

On weekdays, 7:30 a.m. mass was compulsory; Saturday was a holiday, but on Sunday there was 8 a.m. mass and an 8 to 10 p.m. study hall.

Most members of Fordham's football team lived at St. John's Hall, among them an undersized guard named Vince Lombardi. Father Mulqueen was a football fan, but that didn't mean he expected any back talk, not even from the linemen then famous as the Seven Blocks of Granite.

When a boy was caught coming in past the curfew hour, the cigar-smoking Irishman gave him a choice. Mulqueen could report him to the central office, which would mean a letter home and possibly suspension from classes. Or the culprit could lean over and take some priestly punishment.

Mulqueen's interests included the college band — in 1970, aged 76, he was still handing out uniforms and instruments to musicians — and he had acquired a broken drumstick which was of no further use to the percussion section.

It made an excellent rod for chastisement and it was his usual choice. For more flagrant violators, he also had a length of knotted light cord that whistled through the air with fine effect.

In most cases, a boy preferred several vigorous swats from the prefect to the hullabaloo a report to the central office would arouse.

As Father Mulqueen approached the dorm that night, all was quiet. He opened the front door and looked toward the stairs leading up to the sleeping quarters.

Creeping down the staircase, shoes in hand, were a pair of familiar figures. The larger one was a substitute on the football team, Jim Lawlor. Beside him was his roommate, the future Packers' coach.

The priest walked briskly toward the stairs. Lombardi and his roommate looked sheepishly down. Then they turned and started back to their room — still holding their shoes, still tiptoeing.

Mulqueen was a disciplinarian but he was also Irish. The sight of those two large young men minicing along the corridor, pretending they hadn't planned to sneak out, struck him as hilarious.

He had the best laugh he'd enjoyed in weeks and didn't have the heart to use his light cord — or even the broken drumstick.

Lombardi did not always escape, however. On another night, Mulqueen learned that Lawlor had been out past the curfew. He strode into the boys' room, pulled the drumstick from under his cassock and gave Jim several hearty whacks.

Vince sat on the other bed, laughing. This time the priest was not amused.

"If he went out, you must have been out, too," he told Lombardi, and began swatting him with the drumstick.

Usually, the future coach stayed out of trouble, but trying to outwit Mulqueen was a game, and Lombardi was not one to remain a bystander.

The priest's favorite technique in controlling student crap games was to stroll about, apparently reading his breviary, listening for the click of dice or the murmur of excited voices. If he caught the boys shooting dice, he would go roaring in, confiscate the money for the mission fund, then lay about him with his knotted light cord.

Lawlor and Lombardi, however, managed to run a regularly-scheduled crap game in their room. They would charge a nickle a pass until they'd built up $10, then get into the game themselves. If they lost the $10, they'd start cutting the game again until they built up another stake.

The game had to be played in complete silence if Mulqueen was around, which took a kind of discipline seldom associated with crap games. Lombardi was enforcing the rule, however, so Mulqueen never caught them.

Fordham had only about 1,600 students in those days, with all but 250 of the boys living off-campus. As one of the boarders, Lombardi knew most of the other students, but he had only a few close friends, mostly other football players.

When Vince was a sophomore, the freshman team had a talented guard, Ed Franco, who was later to become an all-America. For a time it seemed that Ed would have to beat out Lombardi to make the varsity.

Franco met Lombardi in an ice cream parlor near the campus. Vince was with his girl, Marie Planitz, the sister of another Fordham student.

"So, you're Ed Franco," said Marie, who would become Mrs. Lombardi. "You're the fellow who's trying to take my boyfriend's job."

She bet Franco a box of candy that he couldn't do it. When Ed became eligible for the varsity, however, Sleepy Jim Crowley used him as a tackle instead of a guard, so no one won the bet.

Crowley and his assistant, Frank Leahy, had perhaps the finest defensive team in the land during the middle thirties. From 1935 through 1937, it shut out its opponents 13 times, including three-successive scoreless ties with Jock Sutherland's rugged Pittsburgh team.

In 1936, Lombardi's last season, the Fordham Rams seemed destined for the Rose Bowl — in fact, the motto that year was "Rose Hill to Rose Bowl." With one game left on its schedule, the team was invited to play in the bowl.

There was a feeling around Fordham that Notre Dame hogged

the football honors among Catholic schools. Fordham had never played in a bowl game. This seemed to be its year for glory.

The Rams had beaten Franklin and Marshall, Southern Methodist, Waynesburg and St. Mary's of California before playing to their customary scoreless tie with Pittsburgh. They had then whipped Purdue, 15-0, and tied Georgia, 7-7.

In 1929 and 1930, another Fordham line had been called the Seven Blocks of Granite — an anonymous Associated Press caption writer first used the term and it caught on. Tim Cohane, the Rams' public relations man, revived the description for the line that included Lombardi. It was the school's boast that no touchdown had been scored by running through those seven stubborn young men, although a few had been made by running around them or throwing over their heads.

All that Fordham had to do was announce its acceptance of the Rose Bowl invitation, but it was decided to wait until after the game with New York University, a traditional rival which the 1935 Rams had beaten, 21-0.

N.Y.U. was only an average team — a rinkydink outfit, Lombardi doubtless called it. It was felt that the Rose Bowl announcement would be more appropriate after Fordham had whipped the New Yorkers.

Fordham usually played its games in the Polo Grounds, but this year the season finale with N.Y.U. was moved to Yankee Stadium so more tickets could be sold. Some 82,000 spectators showed up, the largest crowd ever to see a Fordham team play.

Around Rose Hill, they're still trying to explain what happened that afternoon 34 years ago. Everyone agrees that the Rams had a better team, but it was one of those games where nothing went right.

N.Y.U. had a punter who kept booting the ball to the Rams' coffin corner. Fordham would push and shove and struggle down toward the N.Y.U. goal, then lose the ball around the 40-yard line. Before long, the Rams were back on their two- or three-yard line with the whole job to do over again.

The best Fordham could do was a pair of field goals. The six points would be enough if the Seven Blocks of Granite could keep N.Y.U. scoreless as they had S.M.U., Pittsburgh and Purdue.

But N.Y.U. scored a touchdown. It was some satisfaction that it wasn't scored through the line — the runner swept around one end — but the final score was 7-6, and Fordham did not go to the Rose Bowl.

Pasadena didn't want an eastern representative that had lost to N.Y.U. The Orange Bowl folks were less particular. They were willing to have the Rams play there, but it would have been humiliating to settle for second best. Fordham turned them down.

No one defeated the Rams in 1937, their string of victories broken only by the customary scoreless tie with Pittsburgh, and Fordham ranked third nationally that year. But Lombardi was no longer one of the Seven Blocks, having graduated the previous June 16.

No one who played for the 1936 Fordham team ever quite forgot that loss to N.Y.U. It was an important part of Lombardi's education. It was an example of how a team that's up can whip a better team that's down — the Rams, Tim Cohane explained, had succumbed to an epidemic of "headline catarrh."

Lombardi kept the lesson firmly in mind during a career in which he was both coach and self-appointed team psychologist. The plunge from glory to despair that afternoon in Yankee Stadium reinforced his certainty that the world has few rewards for good losers.

Lombardi hated to lose at anything — it rankled him that he ranked seventh in his class at graduation, while Wellington Mara, later his boss on the New York Giants, was third and Leo Paquin, another lineman, placed fifth. "I'll get you guys," Vince used to say, not entirely in jest, but they stayed ahead of him.

He hated to lose at golf, he hated to lose at gin rummy, he blamed himself — others, too, but often himself — when a team he was associated with came in second.

Second was nowhere. When you came in second you got invited to the Orange Bowl, not the Rose Bowl. In the years that followed the N.Y.U. upset of the Rams, Lombardi played that game over again many times in his mind.

He sometimes indicated that if he could have had his choice of careers he would have been head coach of Fordham — not the Fordham that abandoned varsity football from 1943 to 1946 and from 1955 to 1963, of course, but the way Fordham had been when Sleepy Jim Crowley was in charge and the line was as hard to budge as a granite wall.

If it could have worked out that way, things would have been different. The tackling would have been crisper, the blocking more certain.

And when an N.Y.U. back headed around end with the Rams leading 6-0, someone would have tackled him for a loss and 82,000 spectators in Yankee Stadium would have stood up and cheered.

4

St. Cecilia

When Vince Lombardi graduated from Fordham University on June 16, 1937, he stood out among the 300 young men. He was the only one to wear white shoes with his cap and gown.

A cocktail party psychologist might speculate that this was a sign of rebellion against the established way of doing things or a desire to grab the spotlight. But when a friend asked Vincent why he had set his own style in graduation day footwear, he had a simpler explanation.

"I like white shoes," he said.

The young man carried proud memories with him — his status as one of those linemen the sportswriters called the Seven Blocks of Granite and a consistent four years on the dean's list. He also took satisfaction from the knowledge that he had lived up to his father's axiom, "Hurt is in your mind."

The proof of his ability to play with pain came in the 1936 game with the University of Pittsburgh Panthers. Midway in this second of three successive scoreless ties, Pitt had the ball on the Rams' 2-yard line.

The two lines came together. Al Babartsky, who played on one side of Lombardi, was knocked groggy. Vince took an elbow to the mouth, losing several teeth. But big Alex Wojciechowicz stopped the runner.

Barbartsky could hardly stand and Lombardi's mouth was bleeding, but neither would come out. Pitt failed to score. This was before the day of two-platoon football and not until after the game did Vince take time to get his injury treated. Then Dr. Gerry Carroll took 30 stitches.

"When I got home that night," Lombardi admitted, "I certainly was hurting in my mind."

Jobs were scarce in 1937. Lombardi decided to go back to Fordham and get a law degree. He picked up spending money by playing part-time for the Brooklyn Eagles, a minor league team. He also worked as an insurance adjustor while going to law school.

In the summer of 1939, he had a $20 a week job with Du Pont in Wilmington, Del., when another former member of the Fordham line, Leo Paquin, told him about an opening at St. Cecilia High School in Englewood, N.J.

Andy Palau, who had been the Fordham quarterback when Lombardi was a lineman, was the coach there. He needed an assistant. The job was a step up financially — it paid $22 a week.

For its $22, the parochial school not only got an assistant football coach but a basketball coach, baseball coach and teacher of chemistry, physics and Latin. Lombardi dropped out of law school — he had enrolled partly because his father wanted him to — and settled down to the life of a high school instructor.

He took a summer job as an assistant at a summer sports camp and picked up a few dollars umpiring high school baseball games. In 1940, when he was 27, he married Marie Planitz of Red Bank, N.J., whom he had been dating since his undergraduate days at Fordham.

On the football field, Lombardi was merely Palau's assistant, but he had a free hand with the basketball team. Basketball had never been Vince's game so he stayed up until 2 a.m. picking the brains of other coaches. He learned fast.

During his second year at St. Cecilia, the school scheduled a basketball game with a team from Bogota, N.J., one of the highest scoring outfits in the state. Lombardi decided that the way to beat the Bogotans was to keep the ball away from them, and he issued his orders.

They were obeyed. The final score was 6-1, a figure which was startling enough even in those days of low scoring basketball to get

Lombardi's name on national sports wires. The stalling tactics made the Bogota coach furious, but that was not important. The important thing was that Vince's team won.

In fact, during his eight years of coaching basketball, St. Cecilia teams won 105 games and lost only 57, including a year when the school won its first state championship.

Football remained Lombardi's main interest, however. In 1942, when Palau left for military service, Vince got his chance to be head coach. Father Timothy Moore, a Carmelite who had once been given a tryout with the Detroit Lions, had arrived to be the school's athletic director the year before, and he offered Vince the job.

It paid $1,700 for 10 months, with the chance to pick up a little extra income at summer school. Lombardi was not excused from his classroom duties, but at the age of 29 he had his first head-coaching job.

St. Cecilia was a coeducational high school with about 200 boys. Moore was a football enthusiast, however, and he not only encouraged recruiting of talent but he established a football training camp near Hackettstown, N.J., with the boys going there each Sept. 1 to get ready for the fall season.

Lombardi introduced the T-formation, patterned on the winning offense used by the 1940 Chicago Bears. It was a new concept for high school coaching in Bergen County. His players were small but fast and the innovation made them hard to beat.

Other coaches grumbled about it. Father Moore and his head coach, while sitting in the stands at a public school championship playoff, had to listen to complaints about the new fangled formation.

"You two guys spoil football," a rival coach told them.

As a high school coach, Lombardi stressed football fundamentals, conditioning, discipline. In fact, aside from the difference in available talent, those training camps in New Jersey were much like the Packers' camps in the 1960s.

The coach yelled a lot. He had a low tolerance for error. His players feared his tongue and his temper. But as he built his high school team into a winning unit, most of the boys developed a strong loyalty to the squad and the coach.

St. Cecilia not only played larger schools but usually beat them. Lombardi somehow always managed to get more out of his young players than they had known was in them.

His first year as a high school head coach, his team won 6, lost 1, tied 2 — a pretty fair record but one which Lombardi considered unsatisfactory. To satisfy him, the players understood their record should have been 9-0.

So they tried harder the next year. His teams had an unbroken string of 25 victories before Union Hill's boys tied St. Cecilia. The team went on to six more victories before finally losing.

"The one thing I require is a desire to play ball," Lombardi would tell each new squad of boys. "Anybody who doesn't want to play, there's the door."

No one accepted the invitation to leave, but some of the youthful players soon wished they had. The coach not only drilled them to exhaustion and shouted at them but he sometimes jumped into the line at a practice scrimmage and demonstrated how to throw a block.

He hit as hard as though he were back at Fordham and the boy across from him was a lineman from Pitt. Getting hit by Lombardi hurt, but there was no use complaining. The coach would just tell you that "hurt is in the mind" as his father had told him.

"You fellows think I work you too hard from Monday to Saturday," he said to one of his high school teams. "But it will make Sunday's game seem like a picnic." Twenty years later, the Packers were hearing the same philosophy.

Lombardi was an emotional coach. His temper could flare up suddenly. Once, during an argument in an office with a rival high school coach, Vince leaped over the desk and threw the other man onto a wastepaper basket.

As soon as he cooled off, he apologized and the men later became friends. But Lombardi's students felt the mixture of fear, respect and admiration for him that he was to arouse throughout his career.

Before school began one morning, Father Moore saw a girl named Ruth walking along the corridor, crying. He asked what was wrong. She was supposed to go to Mr. Lombardi's class, she explained, and she didn't have her homework done.

The girl's family and Lombardi's family were close friends. The priest knew that Vince regarded Ruth almost like a kid sister. But Moore could understand her concern, even after she'd explained that she'd been visiting a sick cousin when she should have been studying.

"I'm not going in that laboratory," Ruth said.

Father Tim told her not to worry, he'd go with her. He knocked at the door. Lombardi opened it, blinking his eyes behind his glasses.

The priest explained Ruth's problem. Lombardi said it would be all right. Walking back to his office, Moore heaved a sigh of relief. He was sure that, family friendship or no, Ruth would have been in trouble if Lombardi had heard about the missing homework before he understood the reason for it.

Discipline was strict in Lombardi's classes, but it was even stricter for football players. When the team went to its fall camp, Moore and Lombardi spent every Saturday night riding around town, making sure no player was breaking training.

One talented boy was so prone to trouble that Father Moore made him stay at Lombardi's house on Saturday night so he wouldn't be tempted.

Football players were forbidden to smoke. One year, the team's star quarterback was caught with a cigaret.

"Find out exactly when the next bus is coming," Lombardi told him. "Then get on it."

Father Moore called the coach aside.

"Hey, Vince, can't you overlook this? We need him."

Lombardi set his jaw.

"No, sir. If I do it for one, I'd have to do it for all."

The bus came. The ex-quarterback climbed glumly aboard. Lombardi was already on the practice field, yelling advice to his replacement.

5

Back to Fordham

During the early 1940s, when Vince Lombardi was coach at St. Cecilia High School, a student named Reid Halahan got to talking with Mrs. Lombardi on the sideline. The boy made a complimentary comment about her husband.

"Some day," she told him, "He'll be the next Knute Rockne."

Around Englewood, N.J., there were other football fans who agreed with this estimate. Possibly they included Lombardi, who was not a man to downgrade his own talents. But as the years went by, young men he had played with at Fordham went with the pros or to coaching in college, and he was still at a parochial high school.

By 1946, his salary had been increased to $3,500 a year but he needed a summer job to make ends meet. Ray Moore, the contractor brother of the St. Cecilia athletic director, offered him $102 a week as a foreman for the vacation period.

Lombardi turned out to be the best foreman Moore had ever seen. Like Vince, most of the workmen were of Italian ancestry and he got more work out of them than anyone had believed possible. The problem at hand was building a portion of Highway 17 near the Lincoln Tunnel, but Lombardi approached it with the driving enthusiasm he brought to football.

When the 10-week job was over, Moore told him he was wasting his time as a high school coach. If Lombardi would join the construction firm, the owner predicted, he'd soon be making $40,000 a year.

That was $36,500 more than Lombardi was getting from St. Cecilia, but he felt his future was in football and turned down the offer. He was more tempted by the chance at a job that paid $6,000.

Hackensack High School was getting tired of losing to Lombardi's team. Its principal offered to hire him as head coach.

Vince decided to take it, but he still had a year to go on his contract with St. Cecilia. He asked Father Timothy Moore, the athletic director, what he should do.

"Listen, you Mediterranean Irishman," the priest said, "if that's your ambition in life — to make $6,000 — then go ahead."

Lombardi's parents had moved to Englewood to live near their oldest son and when they heard he was leaving St. Cecilia for a public school they would hardly speak to him. His kid brother, Joseph, was on the St. Cecilia football team and he also put on the pressure to have him stay.

Other members of the team deluged the coach with letters. Women in the parish who, as Father Tim liked to say, "don't know a football from a red apple," were Lombardi fans by now. They stopped him on the street to plead with him not to leave.

Finally, he gave in. He called up Moore.

"Father Tim," he said, "you've got to get me out of this."

The priest met Vince at his parents' house, helped eat up most of a large cheese, had a few drinks and much conversation, then agreed to announce to the newspapers that Lombardi would not be released from his contract and so he couldn't go to Hackensack. Vince and the parish was grateful.

In his later years, Lombardi became an accomplished public speaker, but in his early days at St. Cecilia he felt ill at ease before a crowd. When he had to make a speech at a Friday pep rally before one of the high school games, he would get Father Tim to write out some jokes he could tell.

There was no such oratorical hesitancy on the practice field or in the locker room, however. He goaded and cajoled his teams into winning the state parochial school championship during six of seven years.

One year, his boys scored 267 points during the season while allowing the opposition only 19. His reputation continued to grow.

Hackensack was not the only other high school that wanted him, but he was hoping for a college coaching job. His old school, Fordham, had dropped football in 1943, but according to the grapevine, it was planning to revive it.

Lombardi would have liked to be head coach there. When football was begun again in 1946, however, the nod went to Ed Danowski.

Fordham lost all seven games that fall, including a 40-0 defeat by Louisiana State and a 68-0 drubbing by Penn State. There were those around Fordham who did not consider this a distinguished first season for Danowski and felt he could use some help.

So in 1947, Lombardi accepted the job of freshman coach, including the task of recruiting that year's crop of high school graduates.

Danowski's varsity team did a little better that year — it defeated King's Point and tied New York University. But it lost its other six games while Vince's freshmen squad went undefeated. In 1948, Lombardi was moved up to be assistant coach in charge of the offense.

Jim Lansing, who later became head coach, was the end coach. He had attended Fordham several years after Lombardi had been a student there and had never met him. When they were introduced, Vince started diagraming football plays to him before he remembered to say hello.

As a former high school coach, Lombardi knew where much of the talent was hidden in the New York area. He had recruited an outstanding crop of freshmen. By the time they were seniors, Fordham had an 8-1 record, losing only to Yale.

As freshman coach and then as offensive coach, Lombardi was a driving, demanding leader. He worked long hours, then spent the evening talking football.

With Vince coaching the offense in 1948, the team averaged 20.2 points a game, compared with 6.3 the year before. On the last game of the year, he got revenge for that defeat to N.Y.U. in 1936 which had kept him from playing in the Rose Bowl. The Rams had won only two and lost six going into that game, but Lombardi had a talk with them and they whipped N.Y.U. 26-0.

Suggestions were heard around Fordham that the wrong man was head coach. Danowski also had his backers, however, and when some of Ed's detractors approached Lombardi, he turned them down.

Replacing Danowski would cause hard feelings and split campus opinion. Lombardi felt some loyalty to the coach, but he felt even more to Fordham and he had no intention of being the cause of a row.

Besides, there were signs that Fordham would soon de-emphasize football. It was not until after the 1954 season that the school abandoned it for a 10-year stretch, but opinion was growing among the Jesuits that the school could no longer afford to be a major football power.

Lombardi began to look around for another job. He telephoned Tim Cohane, the former Fordham public relations man who was now a sportswriter, and asked if he knew of an opening.

Cohane happened to meet Col. Earl "Red" Blaik on to way to a meeting in the Baltimore Hotel and was told that Army was losing its line coach, Sid Gilman.

Two-platoon football was now in fashion and Blaik wanted a second line coach. He had hired Murray Warmath for the defense, but he was looking for a man to handle the offense.

Cohane remembered his conversation with Lombardi. He suggested his name to the Army coach.

"He's smart, tough, a hard worker and a leader," Tim said. "I think he's your kind of cat."

"Send him to me," the Colonel ordered.

Steven Owen, the New York Giants coach, had also told Blaik about Lombardi. Vince drove up the Hudson to West Point. A few days later, Cohane called the Colonel. Blaik said he had hired him.

"He's all right," Blaik said, then added his summary of the Lombardi character: "He's a rough soul."

6

Vince and Col. Blaik

Vince Lombardi was influenced by his father, then by the strict discipline of parochial schools and Fordham, and finally by the Army, West Point and Col. Earl Blaik.

As a coach at St. Cecilia and, to a lesser extent, at Fordham, Lombardi had been the stern but fair father figure. Now it appeared that he had need for a model to emulate, too. Blaik filled that role.

The Colonel's hero was Gen. Douglas MacArthur, whose philosophy — "there is no substitute for victory" — he tried to adapt to the football field. Lombardi imitated Blaik who imitated MacArthur, although in both instances the imitations were something less than lavish.

As an assistant coach at West Point, Lombardi had a squad of young men who were trained to accept discipline without arguing and to obey orders without question. Vince had always been striving for such military precision among his players so the Army team suited him fine.

His language and tone of voice were often more suited to a top sergeant addressing raw recruits than a civilian speaking to future officers and gentlemen, however. Blaik sometimes tried to get his assistant to lower the decibles and to choose more dignified adjectives.

Lombardi would try to remember. He got in the habit of calling every player "mister," as West Point protocol required, but if someone missed a block or fumbled the ball he was apt to forget that the culprit might some day become chief of staff.

The Brooklyn accent and rough hewn exterior did not quite fit into the West Point atmosphere, but Blaik learned to respect his loud and emotional aide. So did the players. As for the Army brass, some of the officers winced when they walked downwind from a practice that was not going well. But the team was on its way to a 9-0 season, including a 39-0 victory over Navy, so there could be no serious complaint.

Since the first soldiers took the field armed with clubs, military men have understood there is no glory in being a good loser and that an Army that comes in second has not accomplished its job.

So Lombardi's way and the Army way dovetailed in many respects. But like MacArthur, Blaik felt that a war or a football game should be conducted not only successfully but with a certain flair.

"Vince," he would say, "we just don't do it that way at West Point. You can't talk to cadets that way."

Lombardi would accept the advice. He would manage to live up to it until the next time an Army back zigged when he should have zagged or a guard who was supposed to block to the right moved left. The Lombardi would dip into his pre-West Point vocabulary again.

"He has a vile temper," Blaik complained. "He becomes profane on the field."

But Lombardi made hard-nosed football players out of those future gentlemen in shoulder pads and it is hard to argue with a 9-0 season. Before long, Vince had been promoted from coach of the offensive line to full responsibility for the team's offensive platoon.

The Colonel found himself admiring his assistant, and liking him. He showed him off in the Union League Club. He even entrusted him with the high honor of taking the game films to the Waldorf Towers.

Having won World War II, straightened out the Japanese and then been fired by President Truman for mixing politics with his war against the Chinese and North Koreans, Gen. MacArthur was now an old soldier, fading gloriously away high above Park Avenue.

MacArthur was a West Pointer with a warm spot in his heart for the Army team, particularly if it could beat Navy. It would have been unseemly for a living monument to visit the stadium in person, and it was impractical for Army to schedule its games in the Waldorf lobby, so Lombardi was sometimes dispatched with game films to view in the Towers suite where MacArthur was making his bivouac.

It is pleasant to picture them there in the flickering light of the projector, the old hero and the future hero, engrossed in the spectacle of last week's triumph. Lombardi did not agree with Mac-Arthur's politics — Vince was a Democrat and the general, although once considered for the Republican nomination, was essentially a Whig. But the former Brooklyn boy admired the former Milwau-keean's grasp of tactics and each, in his own way, was impressed by the other.

Lombardi had first met MacArthur in Japan when the Army coaching staff made an off-season trip to that country and Korea. The West Pointers had taken filmed highlights of the previous fall's games to show the commanding general, who had enjoyed them very much.

Lombardi's early West Point years were happy ones. He learned to relax enough to play more golf — he had seldom had time for it at St. Cecilia — although playing golf with Vince was seldom relaxing.

He picked up some new axioms from Col. Blaik. "If you can walk, you can run," was one of them. The time came when numerous hamstrung Packers got tired of hearing it.

It was at West Point that Lombardi first met Col. O. C. "Ockie" Krueger. They became friends. Later, when Krueger was commandant of Fort Meade, Md., and considering retirement, he got a call from Vince, who asked him to take charge of the Packers' Milwaukee office. The colonel accepted and later followed Lombardi to Washington.

During Lombardi's first year at West Point, Army and Fordham were unbeaten when they met. The boys Vince had recruited in 1947 were juniors, but now his loyalty was to Blaik's team.

The Rams had scored 166 points in winning the first four games of the season while holding opponents to 43. But this was one of Army's good years and Fordham was outclassed. It was a rough and bloody game. When it was over Lombardi's alma mater had lost, 35-0.

He and his old friend, Tim Cohane, got into a shouting match afterward, with each contending that the opposition had started the rough stuff. The argument was quickly forgotten, however, and Lombardi was soon helping the sportwriter pick a mythical all-

America football team named after a West Point landmark.

The Bull Pond all-America included such players as Excalibur Slime of King Arthur's Knight School and Chuckles Axemurder of Bedlam Hall. Some years later, Lombardi confessed that his all-time favorites were Ugh, the Carlisle guard, and Oscar Upchuck of Old Nausea.

"It took a great deal of thought to pick Oscar Upchuck over Heinrich Schnorkel of Underwasser University." Lombardi told Cohane. "I guess, however, I have always had a soft spot in my heart for good old Upchuck."

With Army teams riding high in 1949 and 1950, there was time for such foolishness. But the late summer of 1951, there was serious question whether West Point would have a team at all.

All but two of the junior and senior players were among 90 cadets forced to leave the academy for cheating. Among those caught up in the cribbing scandal was Red Blaik's son, Bob, the team's quarterback.

Coach Blaik's teams had won 75 games, lost 11 and tied 6 in the last 10 seasons. Now he and his assistants, including Lombardi, were left with a squad of two veteran ends, 19 sophomores and 10 members of the previous year's "B" squad.

The 90 young men had violated an honor system that provided that a cadet must not only avoid cheating but was honor bound to report anyone else who cheated.

Some of those dismissed had been guilty only of putting friendship above the code. Others had accepted help with their examinations.

Various cadets had the same classes on different days. If a cadet brought a copy of an exam from the classroom, others who had the same class later in the week could obtain advance knowledge of the questions.

The football players, who had to combine a full scholastic schedule with practice, were particularly vulnerable, especially since well-meaning friends were often anxious to keep players eligible for future games.

Col. Blaik was bitter about the failure of Army authorities to take into consideration that such cribbing had gone on for years. He implied that the fact that Gen. George C. Marshall, the secretary of defense, who was not a West Pointer had something to do with the severity of the punishment — a court martial trial was refused and President Harry S. Truman dismissed the 90 by presidential decree.

The coach conferred with MacArthur, who suggested the scandal should have been kept within the academy walls, the ringleaders given "a kick in the pants" and the others merely reprimanded. Blaik considered resigning — he had the offer of a $50,000-a-year job elsewhere — but MacArthur talked him out of it.

The 1950 Army team had ranked second nationally, but the boys who turned out for fall practice in 1951 were mostly strangers to Blaik and Lombardi. The scandal broke only a few weeks before the opening game with Villanova. As offensive coach, Vince had to build an attack around an inexperienced line, a third-string quarterback and a fullback who weighed 152 pounds.

The quality of the lost material is indicated by the fact that in the pro draft in 1953, 11 former cadets who had continued their educations at other schools were chosen.

Blaik was heartbroken, but he refused to call off the season. Army got past the opener, then took on Northwestern. Lombardi had been working even harder than usual. For a time it seemed that the effort would pay off.

With a few seconds left to play, Army's sophomores were leading. Watching the clock moving, Vince felt that beating this team from the Big Ten would somehow vindicate the beleagured institution on the Hudson.

But Northwestern's quarterback threw a desperation pass. It was caught. Army failed the stop the score.

After the season was over, with the cadets losing seven games and winning only two, Col. Blaik still remembered how his offensive coach stood on the sideline after the game with Northwestern, tears running down his face.

7

The Maras and the Giants

Much of the enjoyment of coaching at West Point vanished with the 1951 cribbing scandal, but this was no time for Vince Lombardi to leave a man he admired in the lurch. He helped Col. Earl Blaik survive the difficult autumn after losing all but two of his experienced players, then spent two more years helping rebuild Army's football reputation.

Lombardi might have stayed longer, but after the 1953 season Steve Owen decided to retire as coach of the New York Giants and Blaik was offered the job.

The Colonel said no, thanks. He, instead, recommended Lombardi who was younger, more ambitious and a coach who would fit in with the kind of football played by professionals.

Wellington Mara, one of the Giants' owners, had been a friend of Lombardi's since they were classmates at Fordham. But after due consideration by the front office it was decided that the team needed a bigger name.

Pro football was still struggling. The days of lucrative television contracts and guaranteed sellouts were in the future. Besides, Lombardi's scanty professional football experience had been in a minor league and his only job as head coach had been in high school.

So a genial Arkansan, Jim Lee Howell, was chosen to replace Owen. He sat down with the owners to discuss who would be hired as his assistants on the Giants' coaching staff.

Howell wanted Allie Sherman as his offensive coach but Sherman was upset about Owen leaving and wouldn't take the job.

"Well, what about Lombardi?" Wellington Mara asked.

"I don't know if I want him or not," Howell said. "But we could talk about it."

Lombardi wasn't sure he wanted Howell, either. But he was interested enough to travel all the way to Jim Lee's farm in Lonoke, Ark., a long way from Sheepshead Bay.

After a weekend spent talking football, Howell and Lombardi decided they could get along with each other and Vince was hired. Howell believed in giving his assistants considerable responsibility, which suited Vince just fine.

The new head coach said he didn't want "yes men" around him. With Lombardi handling the offense and Tom Landry the defense, he didn't have them. There were sometimes differences of opinion.

"It's like getting along with your wife," Howell said of those years. "You love her, but sometimes things come up you don't agree on."

Lombardi was loud and emotional and Landry was quiet and self-controlled, but Howell soon decided he had chosen his assistants well. He considered both of them brilliant and he gave them a relatively free hand, while remaining the boss.

A perennial argument revolved around the 90-minute practice sessions. Lombardi thought a fair arrangement would be to work on offense for 60 of those 90 minutes. Landry, who would become Vince's perennial rival as coach of the Dallas Cowboys, insisted that the defense needed an hour of each practice to get ready to smite next Sunday's foe.

Lombardi made more noise during such discussions but Landry also got his point across. The problem of fitting 120 minutes of practice into a 90-minute session was never wholly resolved.

Meanwhile, the Giants were developing into a better football team. In 1953, New York had scored a total of 179 points and won three of 12 games. In 1954, with Vince goading the offense and Landry handling the defense, the season's point total climbed to 293 and the number of victories to seven.

Not only the players but the assistant coach in charge of offense were learning. When he arrived, Lombardi discovered that there was a considerable difference between college football and the tactics used by the pros.

He was sound enough on the running game, which remained his favorite method of moving the ball downfield. But he had things to learn about the uses of the forward pass. At first, such players as Frank Gifford were showing Lombardi instead of being shown.

Lombardi listened. Soon, he had grasped the fine points of the pro offenses and had adapted them to his own way of doing things.

It had been the custom for some members of the Giants' front office to speak up on coaching matters, but Lombardi tolerated no such interference. As soon as he got the job he told one of his bosses, Wellington Mara, how things would be run.

"When I have a meeting with my unit, I don't want any outsiders present," he said. "I'm going to have to criticize. I have to feel free to criticize in my own way. I don't want any outsiders to hear that criticism. I don't want any of the players humiliated by having outsiders hear that criticism."

Mara agreed. Lombardi plunged into his new job with his usual enthusiasm. He introduced the Giants to Col. Blaik's version of the belly series; he got the power sweep going and his spirit soared or plummeted, depending on how things went with the Giants' offense.

He drilled his players over and over on the same play until he could hope that they would do it right on Sunday. One week, he spent hours working with a promising end until the rookie ran the pattern perfectly.

On the last practice before the game, he called the play again. This time, the end ran it wrong. With a bellow of frustrated rage Vince started chasing him around the field.

Luckily, the rookie was a faster runner than the former Block of Granite, but even after he'd given up the chase Lombardi was still angry. It was not only that the kid had made a stupid mistake, he told Howell, but he hadn't seemed sorry enough about it.

The power sweep, with a back following blockers around one end of the line, was a favorite of the Giants' offensive coach. There was a right way to do it, he kept reiterating, and a wrong way.

He collected movies of a succession of such plays and ran the film repeatedly for his players, pointing out why the play worked or how it had been botched. He showed them the same play on a blackboard. He took them to the field and had them walk through the play, then jog through it, and finally run it at full speed.

The sweep was essentially a simple and somewhat old-fashioned way of advancing the ball, but Lombardi believed that if the players practiced it enough, believed in it and thoroughly understood it, it would be effective.

New York had not won a National Football League championship since 1938, but in 1956 the Giants took the title. Howell was generous about sharing the credit with his assistants. Lombardi had hope for a head-coaching job somewhere.

Sportswriter Tim Cohane, for one, kept recommending him. He suggested Vince's name to officials of the Air Force Academy, Notre Dame and Southern California. But no offer came. Lombardi and the sportswriter ate together after a Rose Bowl game and Vince wondered aloud about his future.

"I know I can coach," he said. "But the right people never seem to know it. I'm 43 now. I'm not getting any younger. Maybe I'll never get my chance."

He acted like a man who expected to settle down in New York. The Lombardis bought a house at nearby Fairhaven, N.J., near their relatives and not far from Vince's old friends at Englewood. They even purchased a burial plot in a cemetery there. The children — Vincent and Susan — were growing up.

In 1957, the Philadelphia Eagles offered him a two-year contract as head coach. It was tempting to a man who was beginning to notice his birthdays, even though, with the possible exception of the Packers, the Eagles were the worst team in the league.

Lombardi said he'd need five years to develop a winner there. The Eagles were willing to compromise and offered a three-year contract. Vince said it was either five years or no deal. The Philadelphians went home. Another season started, with Lombardi still an assistant coach.

The Giants won the Eastern Division in 1958, tied the Colts in the playoff, then lost, 23-17, in the sudden-death overtime. The off-season football rumors began and, as usual, Vince's name kept cropping up.

According to the scuttlebutt, he had offers from numerous colleges. West Point was not among them — the Army had decided

Blaik's successor should be an Army type. Vince considered several jobs, but they were either at colleges that were too small or were de-emphasizing football.

A more interesting offer came from Green Bay. Lombardi had never been to that city before, but he flew out to talk with the executive commitee.

Then he called his old friend from St. Cecilia, Father Tim Moore, and told him he was going to take the job of coach and general manager.

"How long is the contract, Vince?"

"Five years."

"Don't take it. Ask them for a two-year contract. Howell is about to retire. If you tie yourself up for five years, you'll never get back to New York."

"They won only one game out of 12 last year," Lombardi said. "I've got to have five years. It might take me two years to win a game. Then nobody will want me."

8

A Date with Destiny

Since 1919, when the Green Bay Packers won 10 games but lost the season finale to the Beloit Fairies, there had been both triumphs and crises for the team which Vince Lombardi took over in 1959.

Green Bay joined what became the National Football League in 1921, competing against teams from Decatur, Akron, Canton, Dayton, Rock Island, Rochester and Columbus as well as a few larger communities. It is indicative of pro football's financial condition then that the Columbus team was called the Panhandlers.

The Packers staggered through the early years like a hungover fullback with a muscle pull. Earl "Curly" Lambeau was the coach, manager and star ballcarrier, his highest paid regular was a Boy Scout director and it was possible to become part-owner of the Packers by paying $5 and agreeing to buy six season tickets.

Decatur's team survived by moving to Chicago, other N.F.L. teams came and went, but somehow Green Bay hung on, mostly through the efforts of Lambeau and the rest of the committee known as the Hungry Five. In 1927, the team finished second to the New York Giants, whose franchise had been worth exactly $500 not long before.

Green Bay won its first N.F.L. championship in 1929 with a team that included Cal Hubbard, Mike Michalske and a Pottsville (Pa.) youth, John McNally, who is best remembered as Johnny Blood.

In 1930, the team added Arnie Herber, a halfback who could throw a 60-yard pass, and won a second title. It added an unprecedented third in a row the next year. Fan enthusiasm was high but the times were low. When the Packers combined a so-so season with an inability to pay a court award to an injured fan, the team went into bankruptcy in 1933.

The Hungry Five reorganized the club, Lambeau recruited such stars as Don Hutson, Cecil Isbell and Clarke Hinkle and the Packers won titles in 1936, 1939 and 1944. Then pro football began to move into an era of bigger budgets and it was a new kind of ball game.

Lambeau was still coach but his executive committee had expanded to 13 and differences of opinion arose. The All-America Football Conference had been organized and was bidding against the N.F.L. for players. As a nonprofit organization from a comparatively small city, the Packers found it difficult to compete.

The 1947 team had a 6-5-1 record, which was considered disappointing. It turned out, however, that this was the last time Green Bay won more game than it lost until Lombardi arrived.

After a 2-10 season in 1949, only an intrasquad game benefit enabled the Packers to survive. The situation was so serious that Lambeau stayed in his hometown that winter instead of following his custom of heading for California's sunshine. Despite this sacrifice, he soon lost his fight to retain control and resigned.

After 31 years under one coach, the Packers tried three in eight years. Gene Ronzani, a former Chicago Bears halfback, lasted four seasons, during which he had the unwelcome help of most of the executive committeemen in coaching the team.

Lisle "Liz" Blackbourn, a Beetown (Wis.) native who had gone from high school coaching to handle the Marquette University team, took over in 1954. Blackbourn came within one vote of being named "Coach of the Year" over Paul Brown after a season in which the Packers won only four games, an indication of how outsiders felt about the quality of his material.

Green Bay won six and lost six the next year, but the 1956 and 1957 seasons were disasters and it was Ray "Scooter" McLean's turn as coach. He announced bravely, "We're going for the title." He lived to regret the remark.

Narrowly winning one game, tying one and losing 10 for their worst record ever, the Packers obviously needed several things to keep football alive in the league's smallest city: A team, money and a coach.

Advice was the only commodity that was plentiful. The suggestion that bore fruit came from Cleveland's Paul Brown and Bert Bell, the N.F.L. commissioner. "Get Lombardi," they said, and he was offered the job.

At the age of 45, he had never had full responsibility for any team except the one that played for St. Cecilia High School. Few Green Bay football fans had ever heard of him. Even in New York he was hardly a celebrity.

Still, he accepted the opportunity only on his own terms. They were stiff — a five-year contract, the general manager's job as well as that of head coach, all but complete authority.

When the announcement was made, a press conference was held at a New York hotel. While it was going on, a telephone call came from an upstate Wisconsin radio station. Would Lombardi take time for a brief airport interview when he arrived in Green Bay?"

"Sure," Vince said.

Lombardi told the New York reporters he was sorry to leave the Giants and his hometown, but added:

"I knew it was time to make a move if I ever was going to make one. It is a challenge."

A few days after signing his contract on Jan. 28, 1959, he flew to Green Bay. At the airport, he was met by some of the Hungry Five and other important men.

Surrounding the coach they'd hired, they started to lead him away. A man carrying a tape recorder tugged at Vince's sleeve. Members of the entourage brushed him aside. This was not the proper time to bother Vince, someone said.

The voice was not Lombardi's. And so, it was quickly made plain, the decision didn't count.

"I promised this man an interview," he said. "He's going to get it."

And he did, while the executive committeemen waited, having had their first taste of life with Lombardi. As a former high school teacher, however, Lombardi knew that a lesson must be repeated until it is fully assimilated. An hour or two later, he explained to the club's board of directors what their new role would be.

"I want it understood," he said, "that I'm in complete command."

Not since Lambeau's early days had the Packers been under the total control of one man. Not since then had the club been a winner. Around Green Bay there was hope that these two facts were not a mere coincidence.

It was plain that the new coach had already cut off his line of retreat because grasping all the responsibility entitled him to all the blame if things went wrong.

True, he had a five-year contract. The way things had been going, the Packers might not be able to afford to boot him out before the 1963 season ended even if the team didn't win a game. But the fact remained that Lombardi was out on a limb almost as soon as his plane touched down at Green Bay, and he was out there by himself.

The month was February. The season was seven months away. But the Packers' new leader plunged into his job at full throttle.

Before he had been in Green Bay 12 hours, he had given his nominal bosses a lesson in deportment, hired two assistant coaches — Phil Bengtson and Red Cochran — helped his wife rent a house, started work on signing the team's first draft choice, dealt with decisions in the club's office and submitted to numerous interviews with a patience which did not prove inexhaustible.

And thus passed the morning and the evening of the first day. Then Lombardi rested. But on the second day he was back at work.

"If you want Vince," visitors were told, "you'll find him watching the movies."

The film he was watching did not star John Wayne or even one of the coach's television favorites, Yogi Bear. It featured a number of muscular young men wearing Packer uniforms and the coach did not enjoy it much.

He did not like the way the players he had inherited blocked, tackled, ran, kicked or pursued the elusive pass. What he liked least were the statistics — 393 points scored by the opponents to 193 for Green Bay's 1958 representatives, the 1-10-1 total results.

Shots of that midseason game with the Colts gave him particular reason to wonder if he should have stayed in New York, waiting for Jim Lee Howell to get tired of coaching the Giants. The Packers had lost to the Colts, 56-0.

It was hard to believe that anyone could lose, 56-0, even if the contest had been between Baltimore and St. Cecilia High School.

These were the players who would make or break Lombardi who was approaching his 46th birthday without having accomplished very much that would be remembered in the world of sports.

It was during this period of agonizing appraisal that one of Lombardi's bosses arrived to see him, first being sure to make an appointment.

"What do you want to talk about?" the coach asked him.

"I just want to talk about the organization."

"I don't have time just to talk," Lombardi said, and that was the end of that.

Such an attitude toward the accepted amenities seemed not only abrupt but abrasive. But to Lombardi's way of thinking he had simply stated an obvious truth.

9

Learning the Lombardi Way

The team Vince Lombardi took over in 1959 had placed last in the Western Division the year before, but in the Fox River Valley "after hours league" some of the players had set records that may stand forever.

When such bachelors as Paul Hornung and Max McGee were described with envy and admiration as swingers, their fans were not talking about the abandon with which they carried a football.

Those who did not swing were inclined to brood. When a team can't beat anyone but Philadelphia, it is necessary to choose one course or the other — moody instrospection or gay forgetfulness.

There is a third way — going into another line of work. Hornung and Bart Starr, among others, had given this possibility serious attention.

Hornung could do so many different things well with a football — run with it, pass it or kick it — that he had confused his coaches. they couldn't decide whether he should be a quarterback, halfback, fullback or kicker.

As for Starr, the fact that he had been picked 199th in the draft did not give him delusions of stardom. The way other quarterbacks — and not very successful quarterbacks, either — were used instead of him did not develop his confidence. Even after Lombardi came, Starr remained a second-stringer.

The new coach had no such doubts about Hornung, however. He resolved the dilemma about Paul's versatility by informing him he was a halfback. Sure enough, that's exactly what he was.

Lombardi tried very hard not to play favorites — perhaps the most widely quoted evaluation of his coaching methods was Henry Jordan's remark — "He's fair; he treats us all alike, like dogs."

But something in Lombardi's complex psyche was attracted to a player who seemed, on the surface, to be the coach's antithesis.

Perhaps Hornung's occasional disdain for rules struck a responsive chord in the rebel that was buried under those successive layers of discipline, perhaps it was a fatherly feeling toward a young man whose childhood had been spent without one nearby; possibly it was merely the respect Lombardi gave to an ability to play best when the pressure was greatest — "inside the 20," the coach was to say, "Hornung is the greatest player around."

As far as rules went, however, enforcement was evenhandedly strict. The enforcement method Father Mulqueen had used when Vincent was a Fordham undergraduate was not considered appropriate, but hitting a player with a fine was as effective as it would have been to swat him with the priest's broken drumstick.

When the Packers' training camp opened at St. Norbert the summer of 1959, curfew was at 11 p.m. Emlen Tunnell, a veteran who had played under Vince in New York, came in the door one night at 11:05. Lombardi was waiting, Tunnell was soon $50 poorer and everyone started checking his watch carefully.

Being only five minutes early for a practice, a bus or an appointment was considered inexcusably tardy. Some of the players turned their watches ahead 15 minutes to what they called "Lombardi time," which differed from Central Standard. As always, the coach had a reason.

"I believe that a man who's late for meetings or for the bus won't run his pass routes right," he said. "He'll be sloppy."

It was all part of establishing the proper pattern. So was his belief that "I've got to have men who bend to me." His players must be an extension of his own personality. They must want to win as much as he did, approach the game with the same emotion — an emotion that was controlled, if possible, but not hidden.

He wanted them to do a limited number of comparatively simple things on the football field, but be able to do them better than anyone else. He had learned things over the years of working for other coaches, of course, but his approach to the game in 1959 was basically the same as it had been when he was hired as a $22 a week assistant coach at a parochial high school.

As he prepared for his first season at Green Bay, he acquired reinforcements, players who gave promise of playing his kind of football.

Tunnell, who had played for the Giants when Lombardi was still an assistant coach at Fordham, was one of them. He was old but wiley. Fred "Fuzzy" Thurston, a journeyman lineman who had not found a home with Philadelphia, Chicago or Baltimore, was another.

Henry Jordan had been a second-string tackle with the Browns and Bill Quinlan had sat out the 1958 season in Cleveland with a broken leg. Lombardi traded for them. He made room on the roster by getting rid of players who, he felt, could not be molded to his system.

One of them was Bill Howton, who had scored 43 touchdowns since he joined the Packers in 1952. He was a good player, Lombardi admitted, but he was not his kind of player, so he had to go.

The coach had considerable doubts about Starr. He was smart and hard working, but he was too gentlemanly and lacked self-confidence. Lombardi kept him, but he obtained Lamar McHan to be the first-string quarterback.

Lombardi was not the only one to entertain doubts in his first Packer training camp. Some of the players weren't so sure they could put up with him.

McGee was one of several veterans who reported three days early, joining the rookies. As long as they were there, the coach felt, they would obey the rules.

McGee disagreed. He left and was gone for three days. When he returned, Lombardi met him in a hallway. He grabbed McGee and started to bang his head against the wall, yelling until the window panes rattled.

"I'm not going to play for this thus-and-so," Max said when the flurry was over. "He's a madman."

An hour later, still boiling, McGee ran into the coach on the way to a squad meeting. Lombardi's mind was on what he was going to say there. He slapped McGee on the back.

"Come on, Max," he said. "Let's get to this meeting."

They walked along together, the coach unwittingly demonstrating another phase of life under Lombardi — he was quick to anger but a few minutes later he'd forgotten what he'd been angry about.

In choosing the talent that was to carry him through this first Green Bay season, Lombardi made some shrewd trades and a few mistakes. A rookie from Ball State named Tim Brown had good speed, but the club had five other running backs. When Brown dropped a punt in the opener with the Bears, Lombardi banished him to Philadelphia, where he set N.F.L. records for most yards gained in a game and in a season.

All but 12 of the players who started the 1959 season had been recruited by Lisle Blackbourn and a few by Scooter McLean. Some would become stars, but now they were the survivors of a squad which had established the worst record in Packer history. Lombardi intended to change their attitudes.

Jerry Kramer had joined the team in 1958, but for a time Lombardi nearly convinced him he should have stayed in Idaho.

"You look like an old cow," the coach kept yelling at him. "You're the worst guard I've ever seen."

Kramer lost seven pounds in one day, trying to work hard enough to satisfy this man who kept goading and downgrading him. He finished practice. He dragged his way to the locker room, took off his helmet, and sat on a bench with his head down.

Lombardi must have sensed that Jerry had been pushed just far enough. He walked over to him. He reached out and mussed his hair.

"Son," he said, "one of these days you're going to be the greatest guard in the league."

Such tactics were part of his self-taught system of psychology. Anyone could outline plays on a blackboard, he felt, but a winning coach must be able to get inside his players and motivate them.

Lombardi took a special interest in rookies, singling them out for praise, trying to make them part of the team. During the 1959 training season, he decided that one newcomer was hampered by shyness.

Lombardi issued his orders. From then on, the rookie never had a chance to be lonely. When he sat on the team bus, another player hurried to sit with him. On the plane, at the dinner table, a veteran was always at his side.

The rookie didn't understand why he'd suddenly become so socially acceptable, but he blossomed under the treatment. His personality improved, which was fine. His football improved even more, which was much finer.

In his dual role as general manager and coach, Lombardi had to concern himself with finances as well as football. The Packers had grossed only $836,000 in 1958, leaving a puny net profit of $37,300. The margin was alarmingly thin, but the new general manager believed that if the new coach could win, the money would follow.

When the Bears lost to Green Bay in the opening game, Lombardi was not caught up in the fans' enthusiasm for long. The defense had played pretty well in that 9-6 victory, he admitted, but the offense had a tendency to get too emotional.

The offensive team controlled its emotions the following Sundays. It also controlled the ball, with the Packers beating the Lions, 28-10, and the 49ers, 21-20.

But then Green Bay lost to the Rams and the Colts and went into the Giants game with a 3-2 record.

The coach wanted this one. Old friends in the East had told him he was foolish to go to Green Bay, the Siberia of the N.F.L.

This was a game that would prove something if Lombardi could win it. As it turned out, it proved only that New York had a better team. The score was 20-3.

Defeats by Chicago and Baltimore followed, with Starr playing quarterback because McHan was hurt. The Packers had scored 41 points in the two games, however, and Lombardi was beginning to change his mind about his second-string quarterback. He had more confidence in him, and Starr was getting more confidence in himself.

The Packers' record was now 3-5. One more defeat in the last four games and the chance for a winning season was gone. Lombardi had announced that he didn't intend to be associated with a loser, but it looked as if he'd have to get accustomed to the idea.

With Starr still playing and with Jimmy Taylor and Hornung doing most of the ball carrying, Green Bay whipped Washington and Detroit, bringing the game record to 5-5. But the Rams were next. Los Angeles had humiliated the Packers earlier in the year, 45-6.

But the machine Lombardi had fashioned had begun to function and this time the score was 38-20 in Green Bay's favor, and a victory over the San Francisco 49ers followed.

The Packers hadn't won seven times in a season since 1944. Nearly everyone was satisfied but Lombardi. As things turned out, that 7-5 season was the low-water mark of his coaching days in Green Bay.

10

Titletown, U.S.A.

"I'm only here because we win," Vince Lombardi reminded his players as the 1960 season approached. "You're only here because we win. When we lose, we're gone."

The fans had expected little of the Packers the year before, so a 7-5 season and a tie for third place was considered a triumph. It was surprising enough, in fact, that Lombardi had beaten out his former boss, Jim Lee Howell of the Giants, in the balloting for "Coach of the Year."

But now there was hope for a championship. The pressure started to build. The Packers lost to Chicago in the opener, then won the next four games. The fans began to say this was Green Bay's year at last.

Baltimore won, but Green Bay defeated Dallas. Defeats by Los Angeles and Detroit followed, through, and it was time to face the Bears again.

This time, Lombardi's team won, 41-13. It won its last two games for an 8-4 record — only slightly better than last year but good enough to win the first Western Division championship in 16 years.

The Eagles, the team which three years earlier had offered Lombardi a job as head coach and been turned down because he thought he would need five years there to develop a winner, had also undergone a renaissance.

Under Buck Shaw, Philadelphia had climbed from last place to first in the Eastern Divsion, winning two games more than the Packers in 1960. The day after Christmas, the two teams met in Franklin Field with Tim Brown — cut from the Packers because he'd dropped a punt — handling Paul Hornung's opening kickoff.

In retrospect, Lombardi decided that the turning point of the game came in Green Bay's first series of plays. Bill Quinlan had intercepted Norm Van Brocklin's pass. On fourth down, the Packers were six yards from a touchdown and two yards from a first down.

Uncharacteristically, Vince decided to gamble. Instead of sending in his kicking unit, he ordered Starr to give the ball to Jim Taylor.

The linemen opened a hole large enough for the fullback to run through for the first down. But his foot slipped, the hole closed and it was Philadelphia's ball on the five-yard line.

Late in the game, with the Eagles leading, 17-13, the Packers moved the ball from their own 35 to Philadelphia's 30. With 25 seconds left, those lost three points in the first quarter took on new significance.

If the score was 17-16, as it might have been, another field goal would be enough. As it was, Taylor was stopped nine yards short of a touchdown.

After the game, Lombardi could have mentioned Hornung's inability to kick a 13-yard field goal late in the first half, or Max McGee's 30-yard punt which gave the Eagles a chance for their first touchdown. Instead, he blamed himself.

"I made the wrong guess," he said.

The Packers had lost the playoff, but by the end of Lombardi's second season he was already getting more national attention than any other coach. Thanks in part to increasing television exposure, pro football was moving into its decade of greatest popularity. Green Bay was off the beaten track but its coach found himself in the spotlight.

He had mixed feelings about it. He had waited a long time to fulfill his wife's prediction that he would be a second Knute Rockne, and when a national magazine said, "He seems certain to become one of the greatest coaches of all time," it made pleasant reading.

But the publicity heated up the pressure, both on him and on his team, making it necessary to keep winning or be branded a failure.

The players could relax between the end of the season and the start of training camp, but there was no off-season for the combination coach and general manager. Lombardi was not complaining, however.

"I'd be unhappy if I didn't have the added duties of general manager," he said in 1960. "I thrive on work. I'm restless, worrisome, demanding, sometimes impatient and hot tempered. For those characteristics, a full schedule is the best antidote."

Rumors that Lombardi would leave Green Bay had begun before the 1960 season started. At the league meeting to draw up schedules for the fall, the Green Bay coach was seen with Wellington Mara, his old Fordham classmate who was a co-owner of the Giants. Some reporters jumped to the conclusion that Vince was going back to New York.

He denied there was anything to it, the Packer executive committee issued denials, and the Giants made the denials unanimous. It was only after Allie Sherman had succeeded Jim Lee Howell as New York's coach that Jack Mara, the Giants president, admitted Lombardi had been offered the job.

When Vince left New York for Green Bay, it was mutually agreed that he would have first crack at the head coach's job when Howell retired. Jim Lee was getting tired of the pressure of trying to produce a winner every fall and wanted to move to the front office. By late in the 1959 season he had indicated to his bosses that one more year would be enough.

Lombardi and Mara met in December 1959. Vince did not say no, although there were four more years of the Packer contract his friend, Father Tim Moore, had warned him was three years too long. It was agreed that a decision would be postponed until after the 1960 season.

By then, the Packers had a better team than the Giants, judging from the standings. Besides the rival A.F.L. was raiding N.F.L. rosters and club owners were very sensitive about contract-jumping. If Lombardi had chosen to return to New York he could probably have done so, but he turned down the Giants job.

If there were regrets at not returning triumphantly to his hometown, Vince forgot them in the hard work of getting ready for a season in which Green Bay was in the unusual position of being the team to beat for the Western Division title.

One of the rookies Lombardi wanted to reinforce his veterans was Herb Adderly, who had been a star of the Michigan State backfield.

Green Bay made him its first draft choice, but the Canadian League also had its eye on the young man.

Lombardi sent one of his assistants, Bill Austin, to San Francisco to sign Adderly. The Canadian representative showed up, too. An argument eventually broke out in a parking lot, which was climaxed by Austin and the Canadian trading punches while the rookie looked on.

When the fracas was over, Adderly put his Packer contract on the hood of a nearby car and signed it, then headed for training camp and weeks of frustration.

Herb had been an offensive back in college. Lombardi decided to make a flanker out of him. He had good speed and he could catch passes. He looked fine in practice but when he got in a game he looked terrible.

Lombardi yelled at him and reasoned with him and, as a last resort, tried to talk to him like a father. Nothing worked. The coach asked Emlen Tunnell, a defensive back with years of experience with the locker room grapevine, to find out what was wrong.

It took Tunnell only a couple of days to solve the problem.

"He doesn't want to be a flanker," Emlen said. "He wants to be a defensive back."

Lombardi saw he'd been wrong. He switched Adderly's assignment and the rookie went on to become an All-Pro on the Packers' defensive team.

The coach had come close to giving up on Adderly, and even his veterans seldom felt entirely secure. "If you aren't fired with enthusiasm over playing for Vince Lombardi," it was said, "you will be fired with enthusiasm." Among other things, playing for him meant devotion to his father's belief that "hurt is in the mind."

Defensive tackle Dave Hanner was reluctantly excused from one game when he had his appendix out that fall of '61. But the next Sunday, 10 days after his operation, he was back in the line with the others.

As Jerry Kramer once pointed out, Lombardi had the highest threshold of pain in the world — "none of our injuries hurts him at all."

Hornung was voted the league's outstanding player that year and the Packers proved themselves the division's best team by losing only 3 games of 14 in the regular season, thus winning the right to meet the Giants for the championship.

Green Bay had won six previous league championships but the game on Dec. 31, 1961, was the first title game to be played there. Banners went up bragging that this was "Titletown, U.S.A." The weatherman did his bit by arranging for several days of subzero weather to establish the proper tradition for future playoffs.

The Army had called up Hornung, Ray Nitschke and Boyd Dowler, who had played only when they could arrange weekend furloughs, but they were back for the title game.

The Giants had a crafty quarterback named Y.A. Tittle and a reputation as a great defensive team. But this was Lombardi's chance to show his hometown what he had been doing in the provinces, and his players made sure there was no repetition of 1960's disappointment in Philadelphia.

Hornung scored 19 points, Starr passed for three touchdowns, the Packers intercepted four of Tittle's passes and the final score was 37-0. The goal posts were made of steel but the fans tore them down.

According to Lombardi's unwritten textbook on clinical psychology, locker room division, players who have just lost should be kept from letting the defeat get them down, but a victory must be followed by the kind of criticism that is good for a football man's soul.

It was hard to criticize a 37-0 game that brought Green Bay an N.F.L. title, but if the Packers expected their coach to be at a loss for words they were wrong.

"Now you're going to find out what kind of men you are," he told them. "It takes a lot more of a man to perform as a champion than it did to get him there."

That meant more grass drills, no doubt, more wind sprints, more shouted criticism from the sideline. It might be the last day of December, the new champions understood, but next July's training camp torture was already looming ahead.

11

The Glory Continues

When a team has won a championship, it has a tendency to get fat headed, Vince Lombardi believed. The ego takes over. Players and coaches are no longer "willing to pay the price." Management is reluctant to break up a winning combination. Every other team wants to knock off the champ.

Now it was 1962, Green Bay had become the league champions only three years after it had posted the worst record in its team history and it was up to Lombardi to make sure that the hazards of winning were surmounted.

Fourteen of the 22 starting players were holdovers from the 1958 team. Several of the other starters were veterans acquired in trades. But when the training season began, Lombardi started explaining basic football to them as if they were fresh out of college.

The Green Bay Sweep, for example, was familiar even to the casual fan. But the coach ran off his films of the play known as 49 or 28 — depending on which direction it went — as if he had just invented it.

Most of the players understood by now that being shouted at was part of the price to be paid for winning with Lombardi, that it was best to sit quietly under a tongue lashing, remembering only to say "yes, sir," when it was over.

Henry Jordan, who got yelled at with a regularity he found gall-ing, once asked the coach: "Why do you chew me out all the time instead of this other guy?"

"Henry, I'm chewing you out because he needs it," Lombardi explained. "He's not the kind who can take this kind of chewing out."

The players' feelings about the coach ranged from hate to affection, depending on his mood and theirs. He was a tough man, coaching a tough team. But his psyche was not that simple. Sometimes he was a softy.

When 300 friends and relatives gave him a welcome home party in Sheepshead Bay after the Packers beat the Giants in the 1961 playoff, his eyes turned misty. When he attended the ordination of a priest, Guy McPartland, who had played on one of his St. Cecilia High School teams he wept openly.

He had an uninhibited laugh — you could hear it across a noisy room — and he passed the basic test of humor by being able to see a joke on himself. He found the honors that came his way now that he was at last a winner both pleasant and amusing. When an ethnic club voted him "Italian of the Year," he inquired: "Where does that leave Pope John?"

The coach liked to tell the story of how he had fined Max McGee $250 for breaking curfew one night and $500 for a second offense a few nights later.

"The next time it will be $1,000," he said, then added: "If you find anything worth $1,000, let me know — I may go with you."

Three years before, Green Bay had been a team without a star, Now such players as Paul Hornung, Jim Taylor and Bart Starr were big names. Around Green Bay, even the linemen were heroes.

But Lombardi continued to treat them like students of the game, and not very bright students at that.

"Talent is not only a blessing, it is a burden — as the gifted ones will soon find out," he said.

"When Vin gets one he thinks can be a real good ballplayer, I feel sorry for the boy," his wife, Marie, told an interviewer. "Vin will just open a hole in that boy's head and pour everything he knows into it, and there's no way out of it. I don't want to watch it."

Lombardi kept seeking for perfection, although he recognized that it was not attainable.

"You will make mistakes," he told his players after one practice session, "But not very many, if you want to play for the Green Bay Packers."

Compliments were scarce, even though the 1962 team breezed through its exhibition season unbeaten and began to compile a series of Sunday afternoon victories.

"I don't want to seem ungrateful," he said in one of his more complimentary moments. "I'm awfully proud of you guys, really. You've done a hell of a job. But sometimes you just disgust me."

Lombardi discovered that he had a lot more would-be friends than in the days when he'd been an assistant coach. He reacted by limiting his social circle, getting a reputation for being aloof. Most of those with whom he felt comfortable were men whom he'd known in the days before he was being hailed as a football genius.

His players were also subject to the temptations of the easy popularity that comes to a winner. He worried about them.

They were in the public eye. They must, he felt, behave accordingly. No standing at a bar, even if the drink was ginger ale. Neckties in the hotel dining room even at 7 a.m.

Looking out of the window of a Milwaukee hotel, he saw two of his players walk down the street with a pair of businessmen who were known to bet on games. They were on their way to dinner at an establishment where other bettors hung out.

"That will be the end of that," Lombardi told his companion. Neither those two players nor any other members of the team were allowed in the controversial restaurant after that evening.

It had taken Lombardi half of the 1959 season to decide on his 22 first-stringers. After that, changes were rare. Only Willie Wood, Ron Kramer, Willie Davis, Ray Nitschke and Herb Adderly had broken into the starting lineups by 1962.

After winning all its exhibitions, the team defeated Minnesota, St. Louis and Chicago easily, with the defense allowing just seven points in the three games. The Detroit Lions led, 7-6, with two minutes to go in the fourth game, but Adderly intercepted a pass, Hornung kicked a field goal and the Packers stayed undefeated.

Hornung was hurt in the return game with the Vikings, but Tom Moore took his place and the team had a 10-0 record when it went to Detroit for a Thanksgiving Day rematch with the Lions, who were in second place.

That game stuck in Lombardi's memory after the season was over. He regarded it as an example of what happens when a team is prepared for one kind of tactic and fails to adapt to another.

The Lions came up with a surprise defense and in the first half they dropped Bart Starr eight times for losses totaling 76 yards. Detroit recovered a fumble for a touchdown and caught the quarterback in the end zone for a safety. At halftime the Packers were behind, 23-0.

The Lions were held to one field goal in the last two quarters while the Packers were scoring two touchdowns, but the adjustment had come too late. Lombardi shouldered the blame — "coaching stupidity" was his diagnosis of what had gone wrong — and Green Bay won the rest of its games that season.

Green Bay's 13-1 record was the best since Chicago had gone unbeaten in 13 games in 1934, the year Vince enrolled at Fordham.

The Packers went on to whip the Giants in the playoff, thanks in part to three field goals by Jerry Kramer, who had never kicked one in a game until Hornung was hurt.

Later, Lombardi was to say that the 1962 team was his greatest. Statistics back him up. In the rating system he used, that team ranked first in both defense and offense when compared with his others. It scored 415 points and allowed only 148.

With two N.F.L. championships in two years and a record of 24-4 over two seasons, the Packers were beginning to feel unbeatable. This was not an attitude Lombardi approved — he wanted confidence, but he wanted them to worry, too, as he did.

But, meanwhile, Henry Jordan had a chance to describe the happy taste of victory.

"We can hold our heads high," he said, "and our wives can go shopping."

Lombardi did some shopping, too. The year before, the club had given mink stoles to the players' wives. Now they had their choice of a color television set or a stereo console, along with a chance at spending the $5,888.57 each Packer got for beating New York.

The coach recognized that many of the wives were survivors of a different era around Green Bay, as demonstrated by a story he told about Jim Ringo's young daughter.

One afternoon of the year before Lombardi's arrival, the girl came home from school in tears. Her father asked what was the matter.

"Daddy," she said, "are you a bum?"

It was hard for a player to answer a question like that in the middle of a 1-10-1 season. When the record reads 13-1, the question doesn't even get asked.

12

Adversity

As Vince Lombardi had discovered at West Point, just when things are going right something is likely to happen.

When he was helping Red Blaik coach Army, it was a cribbing scandal that cost the team all but two of its regular players. The result: a 9-0 season was followed by one in which Army managed to win just two games.

At Green Bay, after a 13-1 season and a second world championship, only one player got in trouble. But that player had scored more points than anyone else in the league for three of the last four seasons. His suspension meant winning a third-straight title would be even harder than the coach had expected.

Paul Hornung's suspension was announced April 17, 1963. Commissioner Pete Rozelle said the halfback had made bets of up to $500 on college and pro games over three seasons. In addition, Rozelle said, Hornung had transmitted information on N.F.L. games that was used by bettors.

Hornung had not bet against the Packers and there was no charge that his betting had affected his play. A Detroit tackle, Alex Karras, was also suspended indefinitely.

Five other Lions were fined. The five had bet $50 each on the Packers to beat the Giants in December so they had won, but the $2,000 fines more than wiped out the profits.

John Holzer, a Green Bay druggist who had been a Packer fan since 1919, wore a black armband when the news about Hornung got out. Lombardi did not go into mourning, but his disappointment was deep.

He had taken a fatherly interest in the talented young man from the beginning of his tenure in Green Bay. He had recognized a hidden part of himself in Hornung and had tried to persuade him to temper his rebellious high spirts with the Lombardi method of self-discipline.

So the player's failure was also the coach's failure. But there was nothing to do but get ready for a season without the team's top scorer, who was also one of the few squad members able to act as a safety valve for the pressure the coach's tactics built up.

Except for Hornung, the team which prepared for the 1963 season was basically the same as the one which had lost only a single game the previous year. It was a remarkable football machine, its members still in their prime.

But it got off to a disappointing start. The Aug. 5 game in Chicago was only an exhibition, but when the champions of the world lost to a squad of college boys, 20-17, it was a humiliation Lombardi found hard to bear.

The coach had some words to say to his players after two University of Wisconsin alumni, Ron VanderKelen and Pat Richter, collaborated on the winning touchdown. He disliked the College All-Star game, he wished it had never been invented, but that did not mean he expected his pros to treat it lightly.

The Packers won the rest of their exhibition games but they lost to the Chicago Bears in the season opener, 10-3. Lombardi's wife watched the game with Mrs. Gene Brusky, whose husband was one of the team's doctors. Afterward, Mrs. Lombardi noticed her companion crying.

"But, Hazel, it isn't that important," she said. "It was just a game."

"It isn't that," Mrs. Brusky said. "It's what they were saying to you in the stands."

Lombardi, in an introspective moment, had called football a game for madmen. He had wanted his players to hate their opponents — but only until the final whistle, when the hate should be transferred to those scoundrels who were next on the schedule.

It was plain that the emotion the game aroused was not all on the football field. Lombardi ignored the crowds during a game — he had other things on his mind — but his wife sometimes worried that he was in danger.

That was the fall that President John F. Kennedy was assassinated. The thought occurred to Marie Lombardi that some nut with a rifle might take aim some afternoon at another public figure — the man on the sidelines who was coach of the Green Bay Packers.

Lombardi was an admirer of Kennedy — the president had once urged him to go back to West Point and coach Army, but it was not an official order, so he could safely ignore it.

Green Bay lost only two games in the 1963 season but both defeats were at the hands of Chicago, which won the division title. The Packers placed second, and their coach had a word for that. The word was "hinkydinky."

As Jerry Kramer was to say when he combined the literary life with playing right guard, only Lombardi could have used a term like that without any of his brawny listeners smirking.

The 1964 season was considerably worse. The team won eight, lost five and tied one, only slightly better than its record in Lombardi's first year in Green Bay.

Hornung had been reinstated in the spring of 1964 and had started his conditioning program early. He had suggested mid-May. Lombardi had told him mid-April. They had compromised on mid-April.

The evening before the Bears game, Lombardi walked into a Chicago restaurant and saw Hornung at the bar with his date. The coach started yelling at him, chased him out of the building, then returned and tasted the drink. It was ginger ale, but Hornung knew better than to bring this up the next day when he was fined $500.

In the 1964 opener with Chicago, which the Packers won, 28-13, Hornung kicked three field goals — one from 52 yards — and made the day's longest run. But Green Bay lost one-point decisions to Baltimore and Minnesota when Hornung failed to kick the extra points-after-touchdowns. The halfback missed five field goal attempts in the rematch with the Colts, which the Packers lost, 24-21.

Lombardi considered a mistake by Bart Starr crucial in the first Baltimore game. With less than a minute to go and the Packers behind, 21-20, the coach sent in a pass play. Max McGee was supposed to run in a turn-in pattern on the play.

The quarterback let McGee persuade him that a turn-out would be more effective. Don Shinnick intercepted.

The Colts' victory helped put them on the road to a first place finish. Lombardi considered Starr a worrier and this was a mistake to worry about. But the coach decided it had been a valuable lesson that made Bart a better quarterback.

"When I survived it," Starr told him, "I knew I'd never let another mistake crush me again."

Before the season began, Lombardi had traded away one of his established stars. According to an account that has become a favorite part of the legend, Vince excused himself and left the room when a lawyer introduced himself as Jim Ringo's representative in contract negotiations.

A few minutes later, Lombardi returned.

"I believe you have come to the wrong city," he said. "Mr. James Ringo is now the property of the Philadelphia Eagles."

Shortly after the start of the season, guard Jerry Kramer was gone, too. He had a series of abdominal operations which brought him close to death and convinced Lombardi that he was unlikely to be able to play again.

Fuzzy Thurston was injured, which meant that Forrest Gregg had to move to guard from tackle and Bob Skoronski from center to Gregg's old position. A rookie from Wisconsin, Ken Bowman, an eighth draft choice that year, took over Ringo's old spot at center.

Lombardi continued to follow his regular routine. His wife described what life was like at home during the season.

"On Monday, Tuesday and Wednesday, we don't talk. On Thursday, when practice tapers off, we say hello.

"On Friday, he is civil. On Saturday, he is downright pleasant. And then on Sunday, Vince feels the game is in the boys' hands. He has done all he can.

"Sometimes you have to poke him to keep him awake in the car, driving to a game."

It turned out that, among other things, Kramer was being troubled by slivers which he'd been carrying in his body since a boyhood accident. A reporter talked to the physician who was handling the case.

When the account of the interview appeared in print, Lombardi was furious. He had issued orders that he would do the talking about Kramer.

"What kind of a friend of the Packers are you?" he demanded of the newspaperman.

It was a frustrating year all around, with the Packers' second-place finish no consolation. The experts began to behave as if the Lombardi era of excellence was all but over.

Despite the disappointing 8-5-1 record, it was pointed out, it had been quite a remarkable period while it lasted. Since 1958, Green Bay had won more games than any other team in the league. As coach, Lombardi had close to a .750 record.

Of course those days were gone, the experts implied. Too many of the stars he had developed since his arrival in 1959 were getting old. First the Bears, then the Colts had proved that Green Bay could be pushed into second place, no matter what Lombardi did. His team was obviously over the hill.

After 1963 and 1964, the coach's contention that "there is no room for second place" seemed ironic. If second place was hinky-dinky, as he had proclaimed, than what did that make the Green Bay Packers?

13

A Triumphant Struggle

Jerry Kramer was a right guard, the position Vince Lombardi played at Fordham University when he was one of the Seven Blocks of Granite. Kramer sometimes felt this was one reason the coach yelled at him so much.

Another reason was that Lombardi wanted to make him the best right guard in the business, and did. But as the Green Bay coach made plans for the 1965 season, they did not include Kramer.

The young man had undergone no fewer than eight sessions of abdominal surgery. Now he was recovering but it seemed to Lombardi that his football career was over.

The coach did not believe that starters should be chosen on the strength of previous seasons' press clippings. He was usually quick to cut a man who couldn't deliver, although he preferred that someone else break the news to him.

But Kramer had been one of his best players, and when it appeared that the guard's football career was over Lombardi sought the advice of N.F.L. commissioner Pete Rozelle.

"He'll never be able to play," the coach said. "But I want to keep his pension rights alive. How can I do it?"

"Put him on the taxi squad or something," Rozelle suggested. "We'll work out some way to protect him."

One of those who did not accept Doc Lombardi's diagnosis was

Kramer. When the coach said in public that he doubted the guard could play, Jerry described himself as "completely shocked." His doctors had assured him his stomach wall would be in shape for the fall festivities, and he thought they knew more about medicine than the coach.

Lombardi was wrong about Kramer, and for once he was delighted to have made a mistake. Bringing Jerry to training camp had been planned as an act of compassion, but his recovery was rapid. He turned out to be an important part of the Packers' resurgence out of what the coach considered the disgraceful status of second place.

Lombardi had added a leavening of new talent to his veterans — Dave Robinson, a 1963 draft choice, for example, who qualified for a tribute from Vince: "He delights in hitting people out there."

But many of his regulars were past their prime or hampered by injuries. At the start of the season, Kramer and Fuzzy Thurston were on the bench. The offensive line, once a nearly impregnable wall behind which Bart Starr could cooly look for receivers, was no longer giving him sufficient protection.

In the first nine games, the Green Bay quarterback — Starr or, after he was injured, Zeke Bratkowski — was thrown for losses on 43 plays. As the season progressed, Jim Taylor was hurt. Paul Hornung, who had never quite regained his old skills after being required to do penance in 1963, was benched.

In the team's championship years, it had played Lombardi's kind of football, controlling the ball for a series of steady gains on the ground, using the pass only after proving it could move the ball without it.

But now the quarterback too often found himself throwing from fright or desperation, two emotions which the coach disparaged.

The defense was still strong, however. The Packers staggered and fought and improvised their way to some hairbreadth victories. When the team arrived in Baltimore for a Dec. 12 playoff game it had won 9, lost 3. It could take over first place by beating the Colts.

Father Tim Moore, the man who had given Lombardi his first head-coaching job at St. Cecilia High School, drove down from New Jersey to see the game, as he often did when the Packers were playing in his part of the country.

His brother, Harry, also a priest, came along. The Sunday of the game, not one mass but two were held for the Catholic players, with Father Harry Moore taking the first one. Hornung overslept and missed the early mass. He came hurrying into the room just in time to attend Father Tim's.

This was a game for the big money and Lombardi had always felt that Hornung was a money player. He ended Paul's exile on the bench.

It turned out to be a wise decision. Before the afternoon was over, Hornung had scored five touchdowns, the Packers were in first place and it seemed that Green Bay could put up its Titletown banners again.

In the dressing room after the game, the visitor from St. Cecilia slapped Hornung's sweaty shoulder.

"Hey, Paul," he said, "a little religion helps, eh?"

Hornung turned to the priest he called "my confessor."

"Tim," he said, "you're damn right it does."

The season wasn't over after all, however. The Colts, who were supposed to lose to the Rams because they had a halfback playing quarterback, won. The Packers, who were expected to have no trouble with San Francisco, were tied in the last 67 seconds when John Brodie's pass connected.

That gave Baltimore and Green Bay identical records of 10-3-1 and made a playoff necessary for the Western Division championship and the right to play Cleveland for the league title.

The Colts' great quarterback, Johnny Unitas, had been hurt earlier in the season. His backup man, Gary Cuozzo, had left the Dec. 12 Packers' game with a shoulder separation. Tom Matte hadn't been a quarterback since his days at Ohio State and even there Coach Woody Hayes had not encouraged him to pass often.

But Matte taped cards with the Colts' play signals to his wrist and Baltimore defeated Los Angeles, 20-17, despite gaining not a single yard by passing.

Green Bay won the coin toss to decide where the playoff was to be held. As usual, the weatherman cooperated to make outsiders feel unwelcome. Wisconsin was still digging out of a 10-inch snow that had snarled Christmas traffic. The playoff began on a field that had been covered with hay overnight to discourage freezing.

The Colts were enjoying their role as underdogs. The loss of their regular quarterbacks, giving them a built in excuse if they lost, inspired them to play with the abandon Lombardi was always advocating for his Packers.

On the first play after the kickoff, Starr surprised the Colts by passing. The ball was caught by end Bill Anderson, who had been released by the Washington Redskins, sat out the 1964 season, then picked up by Lombardi, who had made stars out of several football castoffs.

Anderson had not played often during the season. Now was his chance in the most important game of the year. He started toward Baltimore territory but on the way he met Lenny Lyles.

The Colt halfback leaped on him, knocking him down and sending the ball bouncing along the turf. Don Shinnick grabbed it and took off for the Green Bay goal line, 25 yards away.

Starr was among the Packers who tried in vain to intercept him. Instead, Jim Welch intercepted Starr. The block sent him to the sidelines with painfully bruised ribs.

The game had barely begun and Green Bay was down by seven points and one quarterback. Bratkowski took over. Late in the quarter he got the ball close enough to have Don Chandler try a 47-yard field goal. It missed. When Lou Michaels kicked one in the second quarter the home team was behind, 10-0.

Chandler was another newcomer to the Packers that season. The Giants had traded him for a third-round draft choice. Don was a veteran but when he renewed his acquaintance with the coach his hands began to sweat and he kept thinking, "If you make one mistake, you've had it."

Chandler's first experience with Lombardi had been as a rookie in 1956 when Vince was the Giants' offensive coach. The kicker and another young fellow, Sam Huff, decided they'd never make the team. They took off for the airport.

Lombardi chased after them, caught them before they'd caught their plane, and told them: "It's silly to go home when you haven't had a shot at it yet." Huff and Chandler went sheepishly back to the practice field at Winooski, Vt.

Both had become fine players with the Giants but by 1965 New York considered Chandler expendable. The Packers, who had lost three games in 1964 because no one could kick a football accurately, were happy with the decision. Chandler made 17 of 26 field goals during the 1965 season. His replacement kicked 4 of 25 for the Giants.

During the week before the playoff, each Packer player had found a sign in his locker: "Anything is ours providing we are willing to pay the price." But despite such inspirational wisdom, the Colts still led late in the first half, 10-0.

Bratkowski was finally getting the ball near the Colts' goal, however. He had a first down on the one. Hornung and Taylor took turns trying to move it the necessary three feet and failed. On third down, the fullback fumbled. Baltimore recovered.

Bratkowski connected with 22 passes for 248 yards that afternoon. In the second half, Carroll Dale — he had been acquired from the Rams before the season — made a leaping catch of one of them which soon made it possible for Hornung to shove his way across the goal line for a Packer touchdown.

Chandler got another chance for a field goal late in the game, kicking from 22 yards out. The ball barely wobbled between the uprights but the three points counted. The fourth quarter ended with the score 10-10, and the Packers trying to get lined up for a 46-yard field goal attempt.

Because this game was for the Western Division title, it couldn't stop there. A fifth quarter began, to end when either team scored. A few minutes later, the Colts had the ball on the Packers' 37.

Matte gave the ball to Lenny Moore. The Green Bay line came roaring in. The play lost a yard. Matte carried it himself the next time. He lost two yards. Michaels came in to kick before the Colts were shoved back any farther. The attempt was short and to the right.

In the Green Bay huddle a few minutes later, Bratkowski indicated he would throw the ball to Anderson. Anderson said that was fine with him and when the pass came his way he caught it for an 18-yard gain. It was only later, after the game was over, that his teammates realized he hadn't known what was going on — he had been knocked groggy in the fourth quarter. He never remembered the overtime period at all.

"You run the plays so often you just go out and do it automatically," he explained. This was what Lombardi had been saying all along, although he preferred to have his ends know they were still in the game.

Dale caught another pass as Bratkowski moved his team to a succession of three first downs. Elijah Pitts, who had felt so lost and lonely in his rookie year that Hornung had gone out of his way to befriend him, was now substituting for the injured halfback. He picked up four yards on second down.

"Field goal!" Lombardi shouted. Chandler started in. Then the coach had second thoughts. "Hold it," he ordered, and it was third down and Taylor had the ball.

"Don't fumble it," Lombardi yelled. "Don't fumble it."

Taylor didn't fumble. He was stopped on the 18. Chandler went in. Starr held the ball. The kick was good.

Green Bay had won the longest game ever played in the National Football League. A week later, after beating Cleveland, 23-12, the players who had been described as too old to last through a grueling season were champions again.

"But suppose Taylor had fumbled," Lombardi said. "I'd have kicked myself all over Green Bay."

14

The First Super Bowl

By checking with a stopwatch, Vince Lombardi discovered that a quarterback has 3.5 seconds, on the average, to throw a pass.

Bart Starr had been given less than this to get rid of the ball on too many occasions in 1965. As the 1966 season approached, the coach gave a high priority to strengthening the offensive team's line.

Steve Wright was one of its members. One afternoon, his voice hoarse from yelling, Lombardi suddenly lost his precarious grip on his temper. He rushed out on the field and began to flail away at Wright with his fists.

Wright outweighed the coach by 50 pounds and was eight inches taller. It occurred to Lombardi when he'd cooled off that if Wright had brought his fists down he could have "drive me into the ground."

Wright did not fight back, however. He stood there, warding off the blows, until the coach calmed down. A sideline observer might have supposed that Lombardi's total authority to hire and fire might have something to do with the tackle's pacifism, but Vince had another explanation:

"He understands me. Fortunately, all of the Packers understand me."

Lombardi said that even while he was hitting Wright he did not hate him or even dislike him.

"I'm fond of him. He's one of the most likable men on our squad. That's his problem. He has all the size and ability he needs to be a great one, but he loves everybody. In a game, they beat on him. Everybody whacks him, and he laughs.

"I guess I was trying to get him to hate me enough to take it out on the opposition, because to play this game you must have that fire in you. And there is nothing that stokes that fire like hate. I'm sorry, but that is the truth."

It was a lesson that had been taught at West Point where Red Blaik used to tell his Army teams: "To beat Navy, you have to hate the Navy."

But Lombardi had known it before he became Blaik's assistant. When he was a combination coach and teacher at St. Cecilia High, one of his closest friends was Red Garrity, who coached basketball at Engelwood High. They played duplicate bridge together, they liked each other; but on the morning of the game between the two schools they wouldn't even say "Hello" when they met in church.

Winning a championship had only intensified the pressure Lombardi felt to win and keep winning. His 1965 team had barely survived a challenge by the Colts — there was no way of knowing whether Baltimore could have won the playoff if it had not lost its two regular quarterbacks.

The Packers had won mostly on what Lombardi called "character," which had something to do with experience, pride and an ability to dip deep into the storehouse of old skills when the scent of money was in the chill fall air.

But it was obvious that the team which he had begun to develop in 1959 was getting old and the coach, a leading opponent of paying large bonuses to untried rookies, reversed his field and became the league's biggest spender.

The established National Football League and the growing American Football League were in the final part of a bitter competition for players, fought with checkbooks. In 1968, the leagues persuaded Congress to grant a partial exemption from the antitrust laws so there could be a common draft of talent. That was the start of a flirtation between the rivals which led to marriage.

But meanwhile there was one last competition. Green Bay came up with its two most sought-after prizes. Donny Anderson, expected to be the new Paul Hornung, was acquired for an unprecedented figure, usually estimated at $600,000. Jim Grabowski, envisioned by Lombardi as a faster version of Jim Taylor, was lured away from the blandishments of the New York Jets by an estimated $400,000.

Such figures are subject to interpretation and some skepticism, but it is certain that spending approaching a million dollars for two untried players was painful for the Packers' general manager, who had once worked hard for $22 a week. But the Green Bay coach needed them, so the businessman segment of the Lombardi personality lost the argument.

A million dollars was considerably more than the Packers had grossed the year before Vince arrived, but now the club was prosperous. Its stadium had been enlarged. A fan might wait years to qualify for the privilege of buying a season ticket. Television revenue had soared and was now divided so that Green Bay got as much as New York.

The Packers' total annual income had climbed to around the $5,000,000 mark. With no owners entitled to profits — the 1,698 Green Bay stockholders were forbidden to get any — the money could be used to improve the business, and the purpose of the business was to win another championship.

The big money going to rookies made some of the veterans restless. Taylor, who had once asked to be paid so much per yard gained over the season, demanded a contract which Lombardi considered an annuity. When he was turned down he decided to play out his option.

Sportswriter Tim Cohane once told Lombardi that the perfect name for a perfect coach would be Simple Simon Legree, a jesting remark that had some truth in it. The resident genius of the Packers felt it was more important to have his players' confidence than their affection. But somehow — for some of them, not all, and then only sometimes — he had both.

Lombardi said that football was a game of cliches — "and I believe every one of them" — but he had an inspired teacher's ability to conceal old truths in fresh disguises. This made him eminently quotable, among players as well as those who write about sports for a living.

His description of one of the basic football skills is an example: "If a man is running down the street with everything you own, you won't let him get away. That's tackling."

Like the seasons before it, 1966 began with training in such fundamentals, along with the usual punishing conditioning program. Each such session was followed by a meeting of the Five O'Clock Club, a gathering of coaches, newspapermen and friends, with the coach holding court, the conversation revolving around him.

He was called the toughest coach of football's toughest team, a combination which had won a grudging compliment from a rival: "You always know what those damn Packers are going to do, but you still can't stop them."

Taylor was past his prime at 31, but he gained 705 yards on the ground that fall of 1966. Starr was having a great year, completing passes for a total gain of nearly 1.3 miles in 14 games.

Hornung had a pinched nerve in his neck — on the sidelines, Lombardi sometimes winced when Paul was tackled — but he showed flashes of his old skills. Elijah Pitts, who played in his place, scored 10 touchdowns.

The Packers clinched the Western Division Championship well before the season was over — it was their fifth in seven seasons. The finale with the Rams meant very little to anyone except Lombardi. He detected signs of slackening off and he had his players doing pushups and running wind sprints before the Los Angeles game.

"You don't have any pride," he yelled at them. "All you have is shame. You're a disgrace to the National Football League."

The players could have pointed out that their season record so far was 11-2, but they didn't. Instead, they went out and beat the Rams 27-23, with Bob Jeter helping the team tie an N.F.L. record by running back a pass interception for a touchdown, the sixth time a Packer defender had accomplished that in the season.

Anderson also scored a touchdown, his second of the year. Lombardi was bringing him and Grabowski along slowly, playing them enough to give them some seasoning.

Anderson had learned that life with the Packers would not be easy, even for a halfback who'd received a record bonus. In one of his first sessions on the practice field on a hot day, he had asked a veteran where he could get a drink of water.

"There hasn't been any water around here in 11 years," the veteran told him, which was an exaggeration but not much of one.

Winning the division title meant the Packers would play in the first

Super Bowl if they could beat Dallas for the league championship. Lombardi showed his men a new play variation on Saturday — he liked to save something special for the practice before a game — and Pitts made 32 yards with it on the first play of the game.

Tom Brown, considered by Lombardi to be "a good ballplayer who is going to be a better one," slipped and fell down, opening the way for one of the Dallas touchdowns. With 74 seconds left to play, the Packers were ahead, 34-27, and it was fourth down. But the Cowboys had the ball on Green Bay's 2-yard line.

A touchdown would send the game into overtime. Don Meredith faked to his backs then moved to his right, intending to pass or run as the situation developed. Dave Robinson sliced behind a Dallas guard, warded off a blocker and grabbed the quarterback who threw a desperation pass toward the end zone.

Brown, the goat of the earlier play, intercepted and the first Super Bowl was two weeks away, which gave every N.F.L. owner time to call Lombardi and point out that the league's prestige was squarely on the line.

Lombardi adjusted his schedule of fines for Super Bowl week in Los Angeles. Violating the 11 p.m. curfew would cost not $500 but $2,500. Anyone caught with a woman in his room would be assessed $5,000.

Some of the players were hurt that the coach thought such emphasis on decorum was necessary for a game which meant not only prestige but $15,000 to each of them.

"It was the biggest game of our lives," Max McGee said. "We were not about to break any rules."

McGee, who had caught only four passes all year, went into the game when Boyd Dowler got hurt. Before the afternoon had ended with a 35-10 Packers' victory, Max had nearly doubled his year total by catching 7 passes, including two for touchdowns.

The game was watched by an estimated 65 million persons, with two TV networks paying $2 million for the privilege of showing it.

Lombardi tried to be gracious afterward. He called the Chiefs a good team. But TV interviewers kept goading him until he admitted that the A.F.L. champion didn't compare with a number of N.F.L. teams.

He hadn't intended to say it and he was angry at himself and at the interviewers — "my game is football, not Twenty Questions," he pointed out. But a little later in the dressing room he managed to avoid calling a reporter stupid when he was asked:

"And now what, coach?"

"Now what?" he said, flashing that stainless steel smile. "We'll now play Alabama to see who's No. 1."

15

Super Bowl II

Late in the first Super Bowl game which climaxed the 1966 season, with the Packers holding a comfortable lead, Vince Lombardi asked Paul Hornung if he wanted to go in.

"No, coach," the halfback said. "It's all over."

A few weeks later, Lombardi had to telephone him and break the news that Hornung's comment had been more accurate than either of them had supposed. The coach had gambled that an expansion team, the New Orleans Saints, would not take a chance on Paul's physical condition. Hornung was one of the 11 men included on a list of Packers from which the new team could choose three.

When the halfback was picked, Lombardi was so overcome with emotion that, for once, he could hardly speak. He cried when he called Paul at his home in Louisville. Months later, he said that this was the saddest day he'd known in Green Bay.

Jim Taylor, the other half of the backfield combination that had helped win four N.F.L. championships for Lombardi, was now with New Orleans, too. But he had played out his option, then accepted the Saints' contract, a method of leaving Green Bay which the coach considered disloyal.

"We're going to miss Paul Hornung," Lombardi said. "We will replace the other fellow."

The coach felt that Taylor's example might lead to a situation where only the money clubs or the fun cities would have the good players." Green Bay, he added after prompting, was not a fun city — "it's a great city."

To replace Taylor and Hornung, Lombardi had his second-year men, Donny Anderson and Jim Grabowski, and the more experienced Elijah Pitts. He also had a rookie named Travis Williams, whose speed brought an anticipatory gleam to the coach's eyes. He added a veteran, Ben Wilson.

When the new players reported to camp at St. Norbert College, he considered a rookie tackle, Leon Crenshaw, a good prospect if he could slim down from his original 315 pounds.

Under Lombardi's prescribed combination of diet and calistenics, Crenshaw dropped 25 pounds in two weeks, then collapsed while standing in the chow line and was hurried off to a hospital. The next day he was back doing grass drills and wind sprints.

"Some of you people are fat," the coach informed his veterans after their first scrimmage. "You're fat in the head and fat in the body. That $25,000 you all made at the end of last year for winning the Super Bowl made you all fatheaded."

The veterans may not have been any more obese than was to be expected after a six-month layoff, but it was true that they were no longer the hungry crew Lombardi had found when he first arrived on the banks of the Fox River.

Not only had their football incomes risen but many of them were earning impressive sums as businessmen, real estate speculators and television commentators, and in a variety of other activities based on their athletic reputations.

Lombardi muttered about how such outside interests were interfering with the goal of winning a third National Football League championship, but he had plenty of outside activities of his own and was not in a good position to criticize.

He was now a national celebrity, his face familiar to every football fan and a surprising number of Americans who ordinarily paid little attention to sports. Some of his players were also celebrities, although on a different plateau.

They had attained the status by winning. Lombardi understood that only by winning again could they remain there.

"We will not defend the championship," he announced at the beginning of the 1967 season. "We will fight for it."

The first fight came early. Lombardi had cornered a considerable number of other teams' draft choices through shrewd trading and had intended to stock up on "futures" — college players whose original class was about to be graduated but who had another year or so of eligibility left.

In part from concern over the dynasty that had grown up in Green Bay, professional football changed the rules before the 1967 draft and voted to do away with such drafting of futures. This meant Lombardi had to use up all his draft choices for men who would report that year.

The coach ran the names and records of college seniors through a computer he had installed near his office and came up with a strong rookie crop — center Bob Hyland and quarterback Don Horn on the first round, linebacker Jim Flanigan on the second, defensive back John Rowser on the third and Williams on the fourth.

Travis was the 93rd player drafted and for a time it appeared he might not make the team. But before the year was out he had scored four touchdowns on kickoff returns, setting a record, and became known as Green Bay's Road Runner, averaging 41 yards in carrying back kickoffs.

The first game was with the Detroit Lions, who won the first half, 17-0. Pitts scored two touchdowns in the second half, Don Chandler kicked a field goal and the game wound up in a tie.

The Packers needed a 46-yard field goal in the game to get past Chicago, then whipped Atlanta and came from behind to win a rematch with Detroit. That added up to three victories and a tie. Minnesota, which hadn't won a game, was next.

But the Packers had not looked like champions and there were nights when the coach would come home, slump in his favorite chair and say, "I'm going to quit."

"Oh, yes?" his wife, Marie, would say, for she had heard such talk before.

"What's the matter with the world today?" he demanded during one such attack of the glooms. "What's the matter with people? I have to go on that field every day and whip people.

"It's for them, not just me, and I'm getting to be an animal."

The Vikings won, 10-7, scoring all their points in the last quarter.

Afterward, Lombardi called a meeting of the 14 men who were still left of the 1960 team. He said it was up to them to help him with the younger men.

"Frankly, I'm worried," he said. "I just don't know what the hell to do."

The next day, however, he was his familiar self. He yelled and swore and threatened to put a number of players on waivers. He waved a chair over one man's head and said he'd like to beat him with it.

This was the Lombardi of old and the Packers responded. They went on to win the Central Division — the league was now divided into four segments — and prepared to take on the Rams, one of four teams which had beaten them in the regular season.

Green Bay had dropped its last two games after cinching its division title. Los Angeles was favored when the Rams arrived in Milwaukee for the Western Conference playoff. Before the game, Lombardi took his text from St. Paul's Epistles.

Paul had said, "run to win," the coach told them. It occurred to Jerry Kramer, who was taking notes for a book, that "Vince has a knack for making all the saints sound like they would have been great football coaches."

Los Angeles scored a touchdown after a Green Bay fumble but then Williams followed St. Paul's advice. He broke loose for a 46-yard run to the goal line. A few minutes later, the Packers scored again on a pass to Carroll Dale.

Chuck Mercein, who hadn't been considered good enough to play for the Giants or Redskins, but had been added to the Packers roster, made a touchdown in the second half, Williams added another and the final score was 28-7.

In the locker room after the game, Lombardi broke off in midsentence, tears running down his rugged face. He knelt down and led the team in the Lord's Prayer.

Dallas had defeated Cleveland in the Eastern Conference playoff. Hornung arrived to watch the championship game — he had retired from football after New Orleans acquired him, but Lombardi was as glad to see him as in the days when he'd been scoring touchdowns.

Green Bay had won three championships in 1929, 1930 and 1931 but no one had won three straight since the league was split into divisions or conferences.

"The Little Sisters of the Poor could have won then," Lombardi said. "I want that third championship. And I deserve it. We all deserve it."

It was 13 below zero in Green Bay on Dec. 31, 1967, with an icy wind blowing through the stadium. The Packers took a 14-0 lead, but the Cowboys recovered a fumble for a touchdown, added a field goal and the halftime score was 14-10.

Early in the fourth quarter, the Dallas halfback, Dan Reeves, threw a pass. The play went 50 yards to Lance Rentzel for a touchdown. With 90 seconds left, Green Bay was still three points behind. It had the ball on the Cowboys' 30.

Mercein took a pass and ran to the 11. He carried the ball on the next play and was stopped on thre three. Then Donny Anderson made a first down on the one-yard line. There was less than a minute to go.

Two more plays left the ball a foot away from the goal line. Starr called a final time-out with 16 seconds to play. A field goal would tie, but Lombardi did not send in his kicker.

He had been criticized for playing conservative football, but now he was gambling. He said later that he felt sorry for the chilled fans and wanted the game to end, one way or another, but there must have been other reasons.

In the huddle, Starr said he would carry the ball himself, aiming for what he hoped would be a hole between Kramer and Ben Bowman. The two linemen slammed into big Jethro Pugh. Bart found just enough daylight showing. The ball was over the line.

It was the most dramatic finish of any game Lombardi had coached. It made Green Bay's second victory in the Super Bowl, when the Packers defeated Oakland, 33-14, something of an anticlimax.

In the bedlam of the dressing room after the Dallas game, Kramer stood before the television cameras and summed up his feelings about the team and the coach.

"There's a great deal of love for one another on this club," he said. "Perhaps we're living in Camelot...Many things have been said about Coach and he is not always understood by those who quote him." Kramer then added: "The players understand. This is one beautiful man."

16

At the Top of the World

There had been hints that Vince Lombardi would retire from coaching after the 1967 season, but few of his players believed the rumor until two days before the second Super Bowl game in Miami.

"This may be the last time we'll be together," he told them. Then he lost control of his emotions and left the statement dangling.

Some of his veterans told each other they would have to win this one for the coach, but after the Packers' victory they couldn't be certain he hadn't simply had that reaction in mind. He denied that he had reached a final decision.

"All these stories about somebody else just might keep me coaching," he said. "I really don't know."

Less than nine years after he moved from comparative obscurity to coach the Packers, Lombardi was the most widely-known sports figure since Babe Ruth.

Lombardi made the rounds. There was the one about the football player who died and went to heaven and noticed a team of angels scrimmaging while a short, stocky figure on the sidelines shouted insults at them.

"Who's that?" the newcomer inquired and St. Peter told him: "Oh, that's God. He thinks He's Vince Lombardi."

There was the gag about how the coach had been injured while taking a walk — a motorboat hit him as he strolled across the Fox

River. There was the story about the night he came home and got in bed and his wife said, "God, your feet are cold," and her husband replied, "Around the house, dear, you may call me Vince."

Lombardi rather enjoyed such stories — he was not above telling one himself if the mood was right, laughing louder than anyone else at the punch line. He was less pleased at some of the nicknames that went around — he was called "the Jap" because of his grin or "Il Duce" because of his dictatorial methods — but he didn't mind the remark about the Italian army.

If Vince had been in charge, it was said, Italy would have won World War II.

In his earlier years, Lombardi believed, his ancestry had cost him some coaching jobs he had wanted. His success was a satisfying triumph over such ethnic prejudice, an emotion he found hard to understand.

As far as he was concerned, his players were "all the same damn color." He judged them not on their pigmentation or genetic inheritance but of how well they blocked and tackled or ran with a football.

Lombardi had waited a long time for success. Now that it was his he sometimes enjoyed it to the fullest. But beneath his often abrasive personality a part of him was introverted, sensitive, even shy. He found some of the necessities of fame annoying, particularly the fact that a casual remark might wind up in print.

He was hurt by some of the things that were said or written about him. After nine seasons, he found the constant pressure of trying to put together one winning season after another harder to face.

He sometimes worried about his health. When he was finally convinced that smoking causes cancer, he went from two packs a day to total abstinence from cigarettes, a decision that was hard on his players as well as him.

He had an arthritic knee and he wore what he called his voodoo bracelet, a copper band, in a half-serious attempt to cure it.

According to the coaching method he had always followed, it was necessary to goad and drive and nag the 40 diverse young men under his charge so they would play winning football. He sometimes got as tired of such tactics as they did.

Besides, where does a man go who has won his third-straight title? Try for four? Or get out and do something else — go into politics, for instance, as was being suggested, or accept one of the job offers from industry?

The rumors multiplied. Lombardi was planning to run for the governorship, for senator. No, he was going to replace J. Edgar Hoover when the F.B.I. boss retired. Or perhaps the Republicans would pick him as a vice presidential candiate, ignoring his lifelong habit of voting Democratic.

Lombardi considered politics, but he discarded the temptation. It was a different game with different rules, and he recognized his handicaps in leaving the familiar world of the locker room for the hazards of public office.

Perhaps without intending to, however, he became the spokesman for Americans who were worried about the direction the country was taking.

"It is becoming increasingly difficult to be tolerant of a society who has sympathy only for the misfits, only for the maladjusted, only for the criminal, only for the loser," he said in a widely quoted speech.

Have sympathy for them, help them. But I think it's also a time for all of us to stand up for and to cheer for the doer, the achiever, one who recognizes a problem and does something about it, one who looks for something extra to do for his country — the winner, the leader."

It is a sports axiom that the publicity mills grind most profitably for members of teams in New York or Los Angeles, the centers for publishing and television. But despite having had his success in the smallest city in the league, Lombardi's own qualities and his players' unprecedented success combined to focus the spotlight on him.

He was the subject of a TV special. His own book, "Run to Daylight," sold well and an account of the 1967 season, "Instant Replay," written by guard Jerry Kramer, sold considerably better. Lombardi was a central figure in that volume. Its author summed up the coach in a widely quoted collection of adjectives:

"...A cruel, kind, tough, gentle, miserable, wonderful man whom I often hate and often love and always respect."

Lombardi was an eminently quotable man, too. He and reporters frequently did not get along, but he kept saying things that helped put football in a slightly different perspective, such as his explanation of why it was not a contact sport:

"Dancing is a contact sport. Football is a collision sport."

As the sixties progressed, the game changed the Sunday afternoon recreation habits of a nation. Millions of men and numerous women spent at least one afternoon a week crouched in front of a glowing tube on which upholstered figures knocked each other down or broke free for triumphal runs.

In a world that increasingly seemed to be made of plastic these young men were using bone, sinew and sweat to strive toward an easily understood purpose. At a time of rising discontent and growing uneasiness, they were a symbol of such old-fashioned concepts as teamwork, the need to rise above injury or pain, a healthy simplicity of purpose.

And if they were symbols, Lombardi was their spokesman. He was not only in favor of such unfashionable notions as discipline and all-out effort, but he had proved that they were keys to success.

The fact that Green Bay was a small city that was able to smite the chosen representatives of metropolises also played a role. In the years of their triumph, the Packers represented not only Wisconsin but rural and small town America.

An article in *Commentary,* a journal which ordinarily does not deal with football or its coaches, put it this way:

"In an age when popular psychology encourages the negative virtues of 'life adjustment,' we have turned spontaneously to a game that places a high value on the traditional, untrammeled American virtues.

"It is a quiet mass movement that tells us much about our sense of what we have lost and our sense of what we need, and Vince Lombardi is its legitimate folk hero."

And so when this folk hero stepped down as coach on Feb. 1, 1968, retaining his title of general manager, it seemed to many who knew him only from Sunday afternoon television that something important has ended.

Something vital had gone out of Lombardi's life, too, although it would be several months before he realized he had made a mistake. He kept himself busy.

There were the ceremonies when Green Bay renamed Highland Ave. for him, the duties of running the Packers' front office, a new part-time career in business — he became board chairman of Public

Facilities, Inc., of Madison, a building firm, a connection that would bring him a gain estimated at a million dollars when the company was sold.

There was a chance to play more golf, to spend more time with his family. There was the familiar task of dealing with reporters' questions about whether he would leave Green Bay.

"This is not a Utopia," he said. "Nothing is. If the opportunity presented itself for me to get some equity, then that would be a different position entirely. But I haven't heard of any angels ready to give anything away."

In talks with friends, a newly relaxed Lombardi said that if he had it all to do over he might have preferred to be a college coach but that pro football had been very good to him.

"I have enough material wealth to take care of Marie and my children," he said in one such discussion. "Now I'm continuing in football to take care of my grandchildren."

But he was certain he was through coaching.

"The pressures were so horrible," he said. "You know, the pressures of losing are bad, awful, because it kills you eventually. But the pressure of winning is worse, infinitely worse, because it keeps on torturing you and torturing you.

"...I felt I wouldn't be able to raise myself to the right pitch for the big games and then I wouldn't be able to raise them to their best effort. I knew I couldn't ever deceive them about it because they were an extension of my personality. So that's when I decided to get out of coaching."

July 15, 1968, the day when practice began, Lombardi had planned to spend the afternoon playing golf. Phil Bengtson, whom he'd hired away from San Francisco when he arrived in Green Bay, was now the coach and the general manager's place was not on the sidelines.

But he couldn't stay away. He cancelled the golf date. He drove to the practice field and watched, feeling like an outsider instead of the head of the family. It was almost more than he could stand.

He had a soundproof cubicle built in the press box so he could watch the games in lonely splendor, for Bengtson was his choice and he did not intend to interfere on the field. But it was impossible to stay away sometimes when the team was practicing.

He was sitting glumly on the sidelines one afternoon when Henry Jordan came by. Jordan had once said that when Lombardi yelled "Sit down" he didn't take time to look for a chair, he had been a favorite target of Vince's acid remarks, and now he had a question to ask.

"Coach, wouldn't you like to chew us out just once more for old time's sake?"

Lombardi managed a laugh, but the gibe had come uncomfortably close to the truth.

17

Who Wants to Be
a Living Legend?

When the man who had been called St. Vincent in Green Bay arrived in Washington, Feb. 6, 1969, he was greeted like a miracle-worker who could solve that city's numerous shortcomings, particularly those which beset a crew of perennial losers, the Redskins.

He was asked for his reaction to the adoring reception. His face split into an expansive grin.

"What the hell's a Messiah to expect?" he demanded.

A number of theories were advanced as to why Vince Lombardi, who had said winning was the only thing, chose to coach a Washington team which had lost more games than it won in each of the last 14 years.

Large sums of money were no doubt a factor, but as Vince pointed out he already had money. A chance to buy a minority share of the club's ownership was important, but in Green Bay he had a degree of control that few owners enjoyed.

The chance to move back East may have had a bearing on the decision. But almost as soon as he got to Green Bay and started winning football games, clubs from that area and others had tried to lure him away and been turned down.

There he had been coach as well as general manager, however. Those offers came before his realization on July 15, 1968, that by giving up coaching he had made a horrible mistake.

He missed it. He needed the tension, the pressure and sweaty camaraderie. But he could not return to coaching at Green Bay without undercutting the man he had chosen to succeed him.

There were critics who said that Lombardi left the Packers' coaching job just in time. Several key players had retired, others were growing old. The team's 1968 record was 6-7-1, the first losing season since Scooter McLean's one-year regime.

But as long as Lombardi stayed in the front office, his coaching record — 141 victories in 184 games — remained inviolate. As people kept saying, it had made him a legend.

And that was another reason he accepted the Washington offer — he didn't want to be regarded as a legend.

"I'm not a legend because I don't want to be a legend," he said. "You have to be Halas to be a legend. George Halas is 74 years old, and he's done something for the game. I'm too young to be a legend."

So here he was in Washington, sounding much as he had when he arrived in Green Bay in 1959. He would be in full charge. He did not plan to be associated with a loser. He did not promise a championship — not the first year, at any rate — but he would have a winning season.

He said it and the Redskins players, who had learned from experience not to expect much success, began to believe it and steeled themselves to pay the price.

The team had won 5 and lost 9 in 1968. Since its last league championship in 1942, it had a record of 126-190-15. Part of its lack of success had come from a reluctance to add black players at a time when other teams were integrating. But even after the Redskins started drafting talented Negroes they continued to lose.

Leaving the Packers did not mean he was disloyal to Green Bay, Lombardi explained in an emotional farewell to the city where he had made his reputation.

"I will be loyal, I will be your friend," he said, "and I hope you will be mine."

He took over a team with some talented members — most notably its quarterback, Christian Adolph "Sonny" Jurgensen, who held the league mark for most passes attempted, most passes completed, and most yardage gained by passing in a season.

Despite all those passes, however, the Redskins had usually lost. Lombardi started seeking reinforcements as soon as he had unpacked. A considerable number of them were men he had known either in Green Bay or in his days as an assistant coach with the Giants.

He hired Bill Austin, who had been his assistant with the Packers for five years, and Lew Carpenter, who had played five seasons with him as assistant coaches, along with Harland Svare, who had been a Giants' linebacker during Vince's New York days.

Sam Huff, another former Giant, came out of retirement to play one more season for Lombardi. Tom Brown, whose pass interception had helped the Packers win the 1967 playoff with the Rams, was obtained from Green Bay.

Bob Long, who had played in three N.F.L. championship games and two Super Bowls under Lombardi before being traded to Atlanta, was brought to Washington to give the coach another familiar face on the field. Late in the season, Chuck Mercein, who had been obtained from Washington on waivers by the Packers in time to help Vince win in 1967, was waived back to the Redskins again.

Before Lombardi arrived, Washington had traded away three of its first four draft choices, limiting the new coach's hunt for new talent. Still, he came up with a gem on the eighth round — Larry Brown, a Pennsylvanian out of Kansas State, who nearly broke the Redskins' rushing record before the fall was over and was picked for the Pro Bowl.

Players came and went, with no fewer than 23 free agents signed. Lombardi kept shuffling and reshuffling the deck to try to deal himself a winning hand.

At Dickinson College in Carlisle, Pa., where the Redskins trained, he pushed them as hard as he had his Packers. The conditioning was particularly hard on such veterans as Huff, who had not intended to play until Vince lured him back.

One afternoon, the squad was doing wind sprints around the baseball backstop with Lombardi urging them on.

"You're like a bunch of cows," he kept shouting. "You're breathing like a bunch of cows."

"Don't breathe," other players kept telling Huff. "Don't breathe."

Huff did his best to hold his breath. When Lombardi was finally satisfied, the big linebacker dragged himself to the sidelines where Father Timothy Moore, Lombardi's friend from his high school coaching days, was watching.

"Tim," Huff said. "I'm dying."

The priest was outside Vince's room one afternoon when three rookies who had been given substantial bonuses by Lombardi's predecessor, Otto Graham, walked in and told him they were quitting.

Moore could only hear one side of the conversation. Lombardi began shouting that "if you quit now you're going to quit in everything you do in life, you're going to quit on life," then went on to lecture them at considerable length.

Later, he told Father Tim that he had planned to cut two of them anyway, but he considered that no excuse for giving up.

"They loved the game a week ago and now they don't like it," he said, "but all three took bonuses. This is an example of the moral code of our country. This is what our colleges are turning out."

Shortly before one of the July sessions began, as assistant coach asked Lombardi if practice could be postponed by half an hour. The players wanted to see the takeoff of Apollo 11, which was heading toward the first manned moon landing.

"What the hell good is it going to do the astronauts or our team if we sit on our fannies and watch them go up?" Vince demanded.

So practice began right on time. Before it was over, however, the coach called the 70 players around him, gave an emotional talk about what the astronauts were attempting, then knelt down with the others and led prayers for a safe trip.

Washington opened the season by beating New Orleans, then lost a close one to Cleveland and tied San Francisco to come into the first home game with a 1-1-1 record. A capacity crowd showed up, but there was the feeling that making winners out of the Redskins was too much even for Lombardi.

St. Louis scored first. Then Jurgensen unlimbered his throwing arm, Brown found holes in the Cardinal line for gains on the ground, Huff intercepted a pass and ran it back 32 yards, so by halftime Washington led, 23-3.

The Redskins had a tradition of losing such leads in the second half, but Lombardi had made sure that these players were in condition. They went on to win, 33-17, and kept the momentum going with victories over the Giants and Steelers to make their record 4-1-1.

There was talk of a championship again, but not from Lombardi. He was worrying about the next game. It was at Baltimore. Among those who watched the Colts win was Vice President Spiro Agnew.

This reminded Tom Dowling, who was writing a book about the Redskins' 1969 season, to ask Lombardi if he wanted to be identified with those who used "law and order" as a code word for repression.

"I'm not for too much permissiveness," the coach told him. "But I'm not for any repression, either. I like discipline. But that doesn't mean I'm trying to say people don't have the right to be free, to do whatever they want to, to picket, to protest, to raise hell with the way things are.

"Behavior is for each man to decide for himself. But you have to have football discipline to be successful in this game."

By Nov. 23, Washington's record was 4-3-2. There was no more real hope of a championship. In fact, the team would have to take three of its last five games to have the winning season Lombardi had promised.

Among the remaining opponents were the Rams and Cowboys, neither of which Washington was likely to beat, but it had a chance against Atlanta, Philadelphia and New Orleans. The Falcons were first. The Redskins defeated them, 27-20.

After the game, Lombardi threw a small and select party at the expensive home he'd bought in Potomac, Md. There were senators, a former supreme court justice, prominent sports figures, along with Father Moore from New Jersey. The priest walked over to the man he'd once paid $1,700 a year to coach at a parochial high school.

"You're really up there now, Vince," he said. "It's not like the old days at St. Cecilia."

"Yeah," Lombardi said, looking around the room. "But then we had a lot more fun."

18

Great Expectations
End in Tragedy

The margin of difference between a winning season and a .500 season for Vince Lombardi in 1969 turned out to be four points. The New Orleans Saints lost to the Redskins on Dec. 14 by 3 points and, after Washington dropped its final game to Dallas, the season record stood at 7-5-2.

That was good enough for second place in a four team division — not much of a distinction, but considerably better than the 5-9 finish a year earlier. Everyone kept pointing out that the 1969 Redskins had won the same number of games as the Packers did in 1959, Lombardi's first year in Green Bay.

With the season over, the players could relax. If they chose, they could let their hair grow — long hair made the head hot inside a helmet, Lombardi had explained as the 1969 training camp opened, and even a mustache was a handicap.

"You could run faster if you didn't have that thing on your lip," he told a rookie, Trenton Jackson, one morning and by noon the mustache was gone.

There was some consolation for the team members in knowing that when July came and the 1970 training camp opened the survivors of the 1969 season could report as winners.

Lombardi had never coached losers. After six months of his regime, the players preferred not to learn how he would react to such an unfamiliar challenge.

For a coach like Lombardi, there was no real off-season. When one year's football ended, it was time to prepare for the next.

He considered the challenge of making champions out of the Redskins even greater than the one he had faced 10 years before. The 1959 Packers had been younger and potentially more talented than the 1969 Redskins.

The chance to draft useful reinforcements had been greater then. Besides, in those days rival coaches were not as grimly determined to cut Vince down to size.

"Second place is meaningless," Lombardi said. "You can't always be first, but you have to believe that you should have been — that you are never beaten, time just runs out on you."

He wanted to instill in his players what he called a "ravenous appetite for success." It was an appetite that had developed in Lombardi during a quarter century of waiting for his big chance.

The record indicated he had made a start, however. In 1970 or perhaps 1971, with the changes he would make, he had hope for a championship.

His Packers had dominated football in the 1960s. He wanted his Redskins to dominate the 1970s. He was realist enough to know the odds were against this repetition of history, but he intended to try.

He could think of reasons why it might not happen — his quarterback was getting old, the competition from other coaches was harder, the benefits of the draft had been diluted by pro football's expansion.

But there was still time, it seemed. He would be 57 on June 11 and that was not old.

His knee bothered him sometimes, but a former athlete could expect a few aches. He groused about his arthritis and was reminded, in jest, that pain was in the mind.

At the San Francisco game in October of 1969, it had been noticed that he clutched his abdomen and turned white, but in a few moments he seemed to forget any difficulties except those his players were having on the field.

In June 1970, however, he began having digestive troubles that could not be ignored. He consulted his physician. On the 27th of that month the inevitable happened — he underwent an operation in which two feet of colon were removed.

It was announced that a tumor had been found but that it was not cancerous. This report was for public consumption — Lombardi did not want his father, who was old and ill, to pick up a newspaper and learn the truth.

Father Timothy Moore, who had shared in so many of his old friend's triumphs, came to Washington to be with him. He found Lombardi gloomy, but still making plans for the season ahead.

Training camp was to open soon at Carlisle, Pa. The coach was required to return to the hospital each week for cobalt treatments. He was planning to use a helicopter to make the trips.

"Don't forget to pray for me, Tim," he said. "Forget the flowers — who needs flowers? But pray."

Father Moore assured him he would pray. Lombardi was released from the hospital in time to go to New York to attend negotiations between owners and players. The players were on strike, with only the rookies reporting to training camps.

Pale and gaunt, he showed up at one session of the owners with a characteristic word of advice: "Gentlemen, don't give away your game to a bunch of 22-year-old kids."

The trip overtaxed him. At La Guardia Field, Marie Lombardi saw how tired he was. She asked an airline clerk to get him on the plane ahead of the crowd so he could relax. But this was not done for some time and when the short flight to Washington was over Lombardi was exhausted.

Mrs. Lombardi collected the two heavy suitcases and started carrying them with some difficulty. A passerby asked Lombardi if he could help.

"You know Vin," Marie Lombardi said later. "He never needed help. But he turned to this young man and said, 'Help me.' I almost cried right there."

That was July 25. The next day, Lombardi went to Baltimore to see his rookies play the Colts' first-year men. There had been hundreds of games over the years — at high schools, at colleges, with the pros — and Vince had wanted to win all of them.

This was his last. Within 24 hours he would be back in the hospital for more surgery, a final desperate effort to win a hopeless battle against the cancer that was destroying him. Still, it mattered to him how the rookies' game came out, as it had always mattered. But Washington lost.

When Lombardi was able to have visitors after the operation, Father Moore went to see him. He found the coach 40 or 50 pounds lighter than before the illness began.

He tried not to show how it felt to look down on the wasted figure in the bed and recall the vigorous man he had admired for so long. He leaned over to hear what Lombardi was saying. It didn't seem to make sense. It sounded as if he was talking about submarines.

"You know how you sink an Italian submarine?"

"No," the priest said. "No, Vince, I guess I don't know how you sink an Italian submarine."

"You put it in the water," Lombardi said.

It was hard for Father Tim to know whether to laugh or cry.

Death came on Sept. 3. There was standing room only in St. Patrick's Cathedral. Outside, several thousand New Yorkers stood quietly behind police barricades to watch.

The Packers and Redskins were on hand, along with other players and former players, club owners, political dignitaries, old friends from St. Cecilia, Fordham, West Point, the Giants, Green Bay, Washington.

The athletes looked smaller and less muscular in their business suits. Without their helmets and shoulder pads, you could have mistaken some of them for insurance salesmen or schoolteachers.

Most of the players sat staring stonily ahead as the ancient ritual of the Roman Catholic Church consigned one of its faithful sons to his God. One of the Redskins was an exception.

Like the others, he had learned how demanding Lombardi could be, how impatient with errors, how loud and abusive he could become. But now this young man thought of how much he had lost with the coach's departure and during the final ceremonies he put his head on the shoulder of the man next to him and let the tears flow.

"If you're going to be involved in it," Lombardi had said, "you got to take your emotions with you."

He had been talking about football, but it is likely that he meant the axiom to extend to other things. If he could have seen the display of emotion he would have considered it a mark in the athlete's favor, as a man and as a football player.

In the days between Lombardi's death and funeral, there were eulogies from President Nixon and other famous men for this son of a Sheepshead Bay meat merchant.

The outpouring of tributes was unprecedented for a sports figure. Before long it brought an occasional quibble of dissent.

Lombardi had been a fine man, it was said, but he had not cured the common cold or abolished poverty. He had been a folk hero, it was said, but many of those who admired him did nothing more heroic on a Sunday afternoon than sit in front of a television set and open another beer.

All he had done, it was said, was coach football. He had done it well, no doubt of that, but what kind of national hero was that?

Red Blaik would have been able to answer such critics or Sam Huff or Bart Starr. But perhaps the answer — a part of the answer — came during the long drive the hearse and 46 limousines made from St. Patrick's to that cemetery in New Jersey where the Lombardis had bought a burial plot when their children were young, success seemed out of reach and Vince was a relatively obscure assistant with the Giants.

The procession started late. It was not planned as a parade. But as it sped through the little New Jersey towns the streets were lined with people who had been waiting for hours.

The man and women stood with proper solemnity as the caravan passed, but the children waved. Many of the boys were wearing football helmets. Some had put on shoulder pads.

They were Giants' fans, these Jersey boys. But they had suited up in honor of a man who, within their limited memory, had represented the Sunday afternoon enemy, the Packers or the Redskins.

He had been a teacher as well as a coach, seeking to persuade by precept and example that the pursuit of excellence was relevant at a time when the mottos most in fashion seemed to be "getting by" and "making do."

Those kids in their football suits were a sign that his life was still an influence on the young he had always been trying to reach.

Perhaps their tribute was the one Lombardi would have valued most of all.

BOOK II

"Someday he will be the next Knute Rockne."

　　　　　　　Marie Lombardi

19

Whipcracker of the Packers
by Joe Donnelly

One of football's greatest coaching records belongs to Vincent Thomas Lombardi, born in the Sheepshead Bay section of Brooklyn 48 and one-half years ago. In 22 years Lombardi has been associated with only two losing teams, Fordham in 1948 and Army in 1951. When he coached St. Cecilia High School in Englewood, New Jersey, the team went through 36 games unbeaten and in Vince's eight seasons won six state championships. The Fordham freshman team he coached in 1947 went unbeaten. Army went unbeaten in 1949 when Lombardi served as offense coach for Earl Blaik. The New York Giants won the N.F.L. title in 1956 and the Eastern Conference title in 1958, with Vince again as offense coach. Then came the most spectacular coup of all. Taking over as coach and general manager of the Green Bay Packers, Lombardi led them from the team with the worst record in pro football to the Western Conference title in two years. That's the record. What about the man?

Sport magazine sent me to Green Bay last September to find out the story behind the record. Not only was I to spend as much time with Lombardi as I could, but I was to observe him in action, talk to his players about him and to some of the people of this unique midwestern football city. Green Bay is unique in the N.F.L. because its citizens own the team. Once, when the Packers were in danger of going bankrupt, 1,698 residents and non-residents from surrounding communities bought shares at $25 each (a maximum of 200 shares per purchaser) to keep the team going. Therefore, most of Green Bay's citizens (almost 63,000) feel they have more than a fan's right to praise or criticize *their* coach and *their* players.

In the week before I went to Green Bay, I met many people who have played a part in Vince Lombardi's life. Let's start with his mom and dad, Matilda and Harry. Or, rather, let's begin with their home. They live graciously on a tree-lined street in Englewood, a couple of blocks from where Vince carved his first coaching success at St. Cecilia High School. On a wall, in the hallway between the kitchen and the bedroom, are pictures of Vince and Marie Lombardi's children, "Little Vince" and Susan. Little Vince is a 5-11, 190-pound fullback who is majoring in pre-law at St. Thomas College in Minnesota. Susan, an excellent horsewoman, attends high school in Green Bay. The pictures showed her in riding regalia.

Harry Lombardi, a square-built short man in his middle-70s whose strong frame belies his balky heart, led me down a set of steps to the basement. This room is a testimonial to many of Vince Lombardi's victories. Scattered about are footballs from winning days when Vince was a guard on Fordham's "Seven Blocks of Granite." On a wall, the parchment framed, is a picture of the line play of one of the epic struggles between the Rams and the University of Pittsburgh. They played three scoreless games in the mid-1930s and Vince was at Fordham for the first two. He was one of the stars of the games. So were Johnny Michelosen, the Pitt quarterback, and Alex "Ali Baba" Babartsky, a Fordham tackle.

Beneath the picture, there is a verse, the author unidentified.
Roared Michelosen:
"It's no go there,
That Ali Baba's a man!
He stopped us cold
And gave us a scare,
So Patrick went spinning over the guard,
And gained no more than a half a yard.

When we went upstairs, Harry went to his backyard garden and Matty talked to me about Vince. She recalls the time when Union Hill played St. Cecilia a 0-0 game in the 1944 Legion Bowl. "After the game," Mrs. Lombardi said, "Harry and I went back to St. Cecilia. We found Sister Baptista there with Vince. Everyone called her The Bap, but not to her face. She had a fierce loyalty for her high school's football team. Now she was crying and Vince was near tears consoling her. I said, 'You didn't lose,' and Vince said, 'But we didn't win.' "

Joining Harry Lombardi in the backyard that extends nearly the length of a football field, I saw neat rows of fruits and vegetables. The garden supplies the Lombardis with all their fruits and vegetables. Stopping at the grapevine, Harry indicated I should try one. The seedless green grape was sweet and good. When I told him so, he smiled with pride. Harry Lombardi seemed a quiet man, not given to lengthy speeches. On one of his hands is tattooed, WORK. On the other, PLAY. But he was to make one speech before I left. I was to recall it many times later, when I found those who spoke against Vince and those who spoke highly of him.

"It's funny about that coaching business," the old man said. "It's not how much you know but how much you're liked. If the players don't like you, they won't put out for you no matter how much football you know."

The Lombardis sent me to see Father Tim Moore of St. John's parish, several miles away. He was once athletic director at St. Cecilia occupying the same office as Vince. In his room there is a framed picture of Vince. "One of the most astounding men I ever met," Father Moore said. "He got more out of a kid who didn't show any sign of ability than anybody I ever knew." To Father Moore, Vince was feared but respected. "He was as uncompromising in the classroom as he was on the football field," the priest recalled. Lombardi taught chemistry, physics and Latin at St. Cecilia, and one day a student, Ruth White, came into Father Tim's office. She hadn't done her chemistry homework and she was crying. The White family lived down the block from Vince's parents. They were good friends. Ruth's brother, Billy, who later died in the war, played ball for Vince. "But there was nothing I could do for Ruth," Father Moore said, "and she knew she was in for it because she had let Vince down. Nobody let him down and got away with it."

Once Vince cut an outstanding football prospect from the St. Cecilia squad because, the boy was caught smoking, something the players were ordered not to do. "We make a rule, we keep it," Lombardi said after sending the boy home.

In 1945, Vince threatened to leave St. Cecilia for a better paying job with a public high school. "I told him," Father Tim said, "that if his ambition in life was to make four or six thousand dollars a year for the rest of his life, then go ahead and take the job. He knew he wouldn't have the free rein in a public school he had at St. Cecilia. So, even though his picture had been printed in the paper as going to Hackensack, he asked me to get him out of it. We blamed it on The Bap, saying she wouldn't let him out of his contract."

That was the same year Vince had just completed coaching the basketball team to its first and only state championship. "Lombardi was no basketball coach," Father Tim recalls, "But here as on the football field he got all he could out of his boys."

"That's true," says Reid Halahan, a member of that championship team. "Vince didn't know very much about basketball. One of the guys had a standard joke. Vince would come in and say he had a new offense. 'Oh, oh,' my teammate would say, 'he's been up to the Garden (Madison Square Garden) again. Bet it's the give and go. We give it to the opposition and they go like hell.' But we learned from him that you had to put out. He had an uncanny ability to make us more than we were. His pep talks at halftime were the greatest. He'd start where he's mad and you can feel it. He'll get so he's screaming and he'll lift you."

Reid had a closer association with Lombardi than most of the high school athletes Vince coached. He served as a counselor for two summers at a camp where Vince was assistant director. There was a time in a baseball game when Vince lashed out a long hit and was tripped, cleverly and apparently deliberately, by the shortstop as he rounded second. Lombardi went skinning along the ground. He got up and made it to third where he roared, "Keep that kid away from me, or I'll kill him."

Mostly what Reid Halahan remembers are the long talks he had with Vince's wife, Marie, as she sat by the baseball diamond. It was usually about Vince, about his college days, his coaching and how he couldn't accept defeat. "I'll never forget," Reid said, "her telling me one afternoon, 'He'll be the next Knute Rockne.' "

Flying to Green Bay, I thought I knew something about Vince

Lombardi even though I had never met him. I knew he had three years of preparatory study for the priesthood, had entered Fordham at the age of 20 and had made the Dean's Honor Roll while there. I also knew he hated to lose and that had been Green Bay's fate the preceding week. After winning all five of their exhibitions, the Packers bowed to Detroit in the season opener, 17-13.

At Chicago, I got off the jet and boarded a DC-3 for Green Bay. I read Vince's scrapbook, which I had borrowed from his parents. In it was a quote from Tom Fears, the onetime All-Pro end who assisted Lombardi in 1959. "When you compare him with Cleveland's Paul Brown," Fears said, "You have to remember that Brown had two years to build his team before he ever played a game back in 1946. But at Green Bay, Lombardi found himself in the most mixed-up situation in the league. He walked into a hornet's nest and got 'em all making honey."

The next morning, Thursday, I saw Vince Lombardi. He's impressive, even from a distance. It was on the Packer practice field, across the parking lot and road from the new, clean, attractive stadium. The Green Bay offense was in the shotgun formation, the formation that Lombardi knew would be used by the upcoming opponent — the San Francisco 49ers. This was practice for the defense. Vince stood behind his quarterbacks, Bart Starr and John Roach, who alternated throwing passes from a position several yards behind the center. All drills are no-contact but the guarding was close. As a pass went complete when two defensive backs gummed their assignment, Vince boomed across the line to his defensive secondary, "Let's hear you backs talk about picking up your man!" The other coaches were talking to their men (Phil Bengston to the defensive line, Norb Hecker to the defensive backs, Red Cochran to the offensive backs and Bill Austin to the offensive line) but across the practice field I could only see the animation of their conversations. I could hear Vince.

"I hear Vince blinks when he's mad," I said to Tom Miller, the Packer publicity chief.

"He also stares," Miller said. "Right now he's staring at you wondering what right you got being here on the sidelines."

The practice session was soon over. "Vince only works them for an hour and 15 minutes or an hour and a half," Miller said. "But

while they're out there everybody moves, everybody's got a job."
When I met Lombardi in person it was downtown at the Packer
office. This is the other half of his domain. Here he's general
manager. On the practice field, he's in cleats and sweats. He looks
like a stubby ex-guard. Downtown he's in business suit and half-
rimmed glasses. He doodles while he talks, using his words sparing-
ly. When I told him I had met Father Tim and other people in his
background, a flicker of friendliness showed on his strong face. The
deep laugh, a Lombardi trademark, which seems to steam from the
depth of his stomach, roared through the Packer office as he remembered the past. ("Vince can't hide joy any more than he can
hide anger," is the way one Green Bay resident puts it.)

Although Lombardi was still busy with preparation for the 49er
game, he granted my request to observe him in practice, interview
him at breaks, and sit on the bench during the Sunday game. He
also extended an invitation to be a guest in his home after the game.
The only request he turned down was to let me in the locker room at
halftime. "Nobody goes in there but the team," he said. "What
goes on in there is between us. But you can come in the locker room
until about 15 minutes before gametime when I'll signal you out."

That was all the personal contact with Lombardi on Thursday,
but I was to learn more about him and Green Bay from others that
day. Noticing that the flags at the post office, city hall and the
Brown County Court House were at half-mast, I asked a passerby
if he knew why. "I don't rightly know," he said. "Excepting if it
could be for old Hawg Hanner up there in the hospital."

Joel David "Hawg" Hanner, defensive tackle, symbolizes the old
(losing) and the new (winning) Packers. He's worn the Green Bay
uniform longer than any other player. In his tenth season with the
club, he was due to miss his first game that Sunday. Gripped by an
appendicitis attack on Tuesday, Hawg had been sent to the hospital
to have his appendix removed. Many people in Green Bay were
aware of his progress. He's a good lineman, a Pro Bowl selection
twice. He's been at his best under Lombardi. When Hawg came to
summer training in 1959 he reported in at 278. Vince tanned 18
pounds off him in a day and a half. Hanner wound up in the hospital. When he came out, he lost another ten pounds after several
days of wind sprints. Hawg wasn't the only one to lose weight.

Others sweated poundage under the withering command of Lombardi. When one Packer veteran complained that it all wasn't worth it, Vince found it out and ordered him out of camp. Billy Howton, then starring at end, was traded because Lombardi didn't like his attitude.

The flags weren't flying low for Hawg Hanner, but for Dag Hammarskjold who had died that week. Still football remained the No. 1 conversation topic. There are two hotels that amount to anything in Green Bay. At dinner hour in The Beaumont, you find old ladies and tea cups tinkling. But the placemat the waitress sets the tea on provides a graphic history of the football team. You can't get away from the Packers in Green Bay. In The Northland Hotel, it's different. Here, the bar moves fast with mixed drinks and Scotch on the rocks.

This is the hotel where Emlen Tunnell lives, one of the grand old veterans of the N.F.L. Now in his 14th season, he's lost some speed and second-year man Willie Wood has taken his starting spot on defense. But when the Packers are defending their goal line or kicking off — Lombardi calls on Tunnell. You can't lose the smartness, it's just the wide open spaces that beat you when you're closer to 40 than your listed 35.

Tunnell answered my lobby call and in five minutes we sank into cab-leather for a ride to De Pere, a town outside of Green Bay. "I hate this town," Emlen said as Packerland flitted by the open windows. "I guess it's all right it you're used to smalltown life. Me, I'm from New York. When the Giants were here they made me homesick. They talked about everything I like. Here, I found one colored guy besides the boys on the team. He's the porter in The Northland and he's 70 years old.

"I'd get out of this town if it wasn't for Vince. He hasn't changed at all from the Giant days except he wasn't the head man then. He's real brash, real arrogant. He's the kind of guy that you have to cuss out once a week when you're alone, but nobody else can cuss him out to me. In my heart, I know what he is."

I asked Tunnell if he could describe what he meant by "in his heart." "That's not orally, " he replied, "that's in your heart. He had to make these guys believe in his way of thinking. He's using basically the same offense he always used but with a few wrinkles.

Mental quickness and mental toughness are what he stresses. All professional footballers are physically tough but not all are mentally tough and that's the edge he drives into his players. He doesn't want you offside or incorrectly in motion. He wants the right defense at the right time. He makes you think about it, drills it into you and it's easier. Baltimore can win sometimes without the mental quickness because they got a great operator in Unitas to bail them out. But Vince gives you all the edge you can get.''

We got out of the cab and walked into Art Beecher's bar and restaurant. The spaghetti's good here, so is the cold draft beer and most Packers like Art because he has the knack of kidding with them about something besides football. You can get fed up with some of Green Bay's fan fanaticism and some Packers do. "Don't make Vince a god," Tunnell said. "Just say that overall he's the greatest coach I ever saw or played for. But part of a championship is also won in places like this where teammates grow closer."

Green Bay's not the hick town that some writers have offered it to be. On a television station you can get Red Foley doing the ancient "Who's on first?" routine and signing off with "Goodnight Momma and goodnight Poppa." But downtown Green Bay is more sophisticated with smiling Jo Treanor doing a sweet job on songs like "The Party's Over" in the Loop. At other drinking spots, the Lyric and the Mayfair Lounge, the music isn't as good nor the singing as sweet and more attention is paid to talking.

At the Lyric, Sal LoCascio, who runs an insurance agency and is father of six kids, talked about Vince and Marie Lombardi. Anybody you talk to in Green Bay, including those people who know the Lombardis personally, agree that Vince's wife had a hard time adjusting to small-town life. Therefore, they believe the reason Vince took so long in denying last year that he was taking the Giants' head-coaching job when that post opened up is because Marie wanted to return to New York. That may or may not have been the reason.

LoCascio knows what it is to be homesick. "My wife and I moved here from New Jersey when I was 26, which was 13 years ago," he said. "You get the good living here. You get a good steak here, better on the average than in New York. But you don't get what goes with it, Saks Fifth Avenue and the like. She's only judged on her social graces. This takes time. Lombardi had the opportunity to be judged as a football coach. His winning team has made it easier for him. My wife adjusted but it took time.

"Lombardi's very methodically built a wall around himself. There's not many people in this city who know Vince Lombardi. With him it's a business deal. Most of Green Bay wants it on a buddy-buddy basis. Vince doesn't want it that way. The guys who've been friendly — Ronzani, Blackbourn and McLean — exposed themselves more. Vince picks his spots. He's doing the job."

Ben Laird, the president of radio station WDUZ in Green Bay, speaks of Lombardi with venom. "He doesn't give anybody credit for knowing anything about football," Laird said. "Hell, this is the cradle of pro football. The new five-year contract they gave him is bad business. You've got a good salesman under contract for five years, you don't rip it up and give him a new one. Anyway, these are Blackbourn's boys he's winning with. Let's see how Vince's draft choices do."

Then there's the other side of Lombardi as seen by Green Bay people. Les Wood, president of a paper company and member of the Packers' 45-man board of directors, says, "We know Vince's background, what he represents. I think most of us like him because of what we know about him. He's wholesome. He's a fine family man, a religious man and then he's a coach with a record of success."

Despite some of the disenchantment with Lombardi downtown, and some of this might quite naturally have stemmed from the tight loss to the Lions the preceding Sunday, practice went on as usual for the Packers on Friday. This is the day the offense works more than usual. Paul Hornung and Jim Taylor were on display with short, quick-running bursts. Bart Starr threw many of his passes up the middle, the area that Lombardi intended to explore against the 49ers. There was a new man on the sideline, a limping Hawg Hanner.

Somebody asked Hanner how they had treated him at the hospital. "Real good," he said. "Except I didn't sleep too good. I went downstairs at 5:30 this morning and asked them for a cup of coffee. They seemed so agreeable so I asked them to stick a couple of rolls in. Boy, you sure won't gain weight in that hospital with that cottage cheese and stuff. But I wasn't much trouble. Jim Ringo, when he was in the hospital one year, he called up the Italian restaurant and ordered spaghetti and lasagna.''

"He would've had trouble," said one listener, "if the doctor caught him."

"I'll tell you," Hawg said, "I'd rather the doctor caught me than Vince."

After the field practice, the Packers gathered in the locker room for a film of their second 1960 game against the 49ers. Lombardi was at the projector. With an automatic release, he would stop at key plays and re-run them. The room was quiet except for his voice pointing out the shifts in the 49er defense. He talked tersely. As the film rolled to an end, a soda bottle standing on the floor was nudged and rolled over without breaking.

"Keep the bottles off the floor," Lombardi said levelly. After a pause, his voice boomed, "I could tell you guys 50 times to keep them off the floor," he said. "But you still put them down there." The heads of Paul Hornung, Jim Taylor and all the rest of the Packers snapped to both sides looking for soda bottles in the dim room. Satisfied that there were no more bottles around, nearly three dozen bodies relaxed again. There was nothing further said about the incident and Paul Hornung tossed it off an hour later as "just tension." But the point is when Lombardi speaks aloud it is as though he were commanding raw recruits.

In an interview later that day, Vince said, "We make few rules. Those we make, we keep." It was almost an echo of what Lombardi said to the boy he caught smoking and sent home almost two decades ago.

That's the tough side of Lombardi, but you won't find a Packer player who'll speak against his coach. Hornung became a celebrated star in the N.F.L. after the arrival of Lombardi. Before that Hornung was a confused all-America who had played every backfield position for the Packers and had done well at none of them.

"There wasn't one player on this team that didn't want to be traded before Vince came here," Hornung told me. "Now the guys want to stay. Now we win. Vince's preparation for a game is one of his greatest assets. One week we might use a play that averages an eight-yard gain. Then he might scrap it off his short list because his analysis of our next opponent's defense has convinced him that this play won't work. Other coaches often stick with what has been successful.

"And he likes to have fun despite all the seriousness. The fellows kid Fuzzy Thurston about being short for a lineman. One day Fuzzy turned to Vince, who is even shorter. 'You don't have to be tall to be great, right coach?' Lombardi gave that deep laugh. We like to see him laugh. He's different than Paul Brown (whom Vince has often been compared with). He gets closer to his men on a field."

Other Packers remember the early days when Lombardi took over their losing team. "He held a meeting," one veteran recalled, "and told us anybody who didn't want to do it his way could leave then because he'd get rid of them. He said, 'This is the way it's going to be and we're going to win games.' And we did, some at first, a lot later."

Here's something," Jim Ringo said. "Nine of the guys on our offensive starting team in the championship game last year also started when we lost our tenth game in 1958 (the year before Lombardi took over). Vince made a lot of boys into men. He tells us, you have to be dedicated. That's what he is. I'm better now. He makes you feel your responsibility as a football player."

Lombardi didn't seek his job in Green Bay. The Packer president came to him. "Bert Bell and Paul Brown were two of the most influential people who recommended me," Vince said. "Paul never told me about it but I know that he did from talks here with Green Bay people." Football people insist Brown and Lombardi are the finest organizers in pro football. They have both coached on the high school, college and pro levels. They are the only coaches in the N.F.L. who also possess the title of general manager. The latter is an important asset. It means they coach with executive power. But the game they play is different. "All together," Lombardi will roar, "get off all together, not like a typewriter," Brown's players are bigger, perhaps stronger. Because of their size, they can delay and then charge. Henry Jordan, for instance, didn't have the size to star with Cleveland, but with his speed he became an All-Pro under Lombardi.

Vince arrived in Green Bay in January 1959. One of his first acts as general manager and coach was to hold a radio-newspaper press conference attended by the 45-man Packer board of directors. "I want it understood," he said, "that I'm in complete command. I expect full cooperation from you people and you will get full cooperation from me in return." It is doubtful that any man who ever headed the Packers spoke so firmly to the board.

Vince then surrounded himself with the four best assistant coaches he could find. He more than doubled the scouting staff, building it to more than 60 part-time or full-time scouts. He instituted a system of cross-check scouting. For instance, Roman Gabriel, North Carolina State's quarterback, was scouted 21 times by 11 different scouts from March 19, 1959, to April 6, 1961. Vince then sat down with his assistant coaches and ran the films of all 12 1958 Packer games. The coaches rated each player's performance. Then, when the players arrived for the summer training, Vince put them through an exhaustive training grind to judge them for attitude. On his second day in camp, he walked into the trainer's room and found nearly 20 Packers scattered about waiting to be attended to for minor injuries. "What's this?" he said in his brisk, loud voice. "You've got to play with those small hurts, you know!" The next day the Packers in the trainer's room had dwindled to two. A.D. Williams, an end, had his foot in a bucket of ice trying to cut down an ankle swell. "How you feeling?" Vince boomed. A.D. hopped out of a chair and said through chattering teeth, "I feel better already, coach."

When Vince had the boys moving the way he wanted them to move, he installed the offense. It was the three-end system. "I do not like the three-end system of offense," Lombardi says. "I prefer a system with three running backs. But we use the three-end system because it is better suited to our present personnel."

The record of success followed the strategy. Ever since, each week of the season has been a small-scale repetition of the battle plan that launched the Packers that first summer. Lombardi starts pacing in the downtown office shortly after nine Monday morning. He's waiting for the films of Sunday's Packer game. When they arrive he joins his coaching assistants at the stadium. Monday is an off-day for the players. The coaches grade the performances of each Packer player. Notes are made of any inadequacies of the opponents' defense that were not exploited. They could be useful the next time the clubs meet.

After the grading, the preparations are begun for the upcoming opponent. Vince and his staff may work until midnight with two hours off for supper. Included among the preparations are film

Vince Lombardi played guard on the 1934-36 Fordham teams.

(left to right) Ed Franco, Lombardi and Leo Paguin pose for a photo on Graduation Day at Fordham in June 1937.

Fordham's legendary Seven Blocks of Granite of 1936 *(left to right)* — Johnny Druze, Al Babartsky, Lombardi, Alex Wojciechowicz, Nat Pierce, Ed Franco and Leo Paguin.

Lombardi instructs a
laboratory class to his students
at St. Cecilia High School in
the early 1940s.

Lombardi's 1945 St. Cecilia basketball squad won the State of New Jersey Parochial
High School Championship.

In 1947, Lombardi joined Ed Danowski's coaching staff at Fordham University.

In 1949, Lombardi accepted Col. Earl "Red" Blaik's invitation to join his staff at West Point, which included *(left to right)* Maj. Joel Stephens, Lt. John Green, Doug Kenna, Lombardi, Col. Blaik, John Mauer, Paul Amen and Murray Warmath.

As the New York Giants' offensive coach, Lombardi *(far left)* helped bring New York one N.F.L. championship and two Eastern Conference titles.

Packer guard Jerry Kramer displays the wood slivers, which he had received during a childhood injury, that were surgically removed during the 1964 season.

Lombardi visits with Chicago Bears' owner and head coach George Halas on the sideline prior to game.

Lombardi and Packer halfback Elijah Pitts enjoy a post-game locker room victory celebration.

While fielding sportswriters'
questions, Fuzzy Thurston
often smoked a victory cigar.

Lombardi visits with his field general, Bart Starr (15), on the Packer sideline.

Offensive tackle Forrest Gregg
anchored the right side of the
Packer line.

Henry Jordan (74) and Willie Davis (87) were brought in from Cleveland in a trade
to strengthen the Packer defense.

Fuzzy Thurston (63) leads the way for fullback Jim Taylor on a sweep against the Detroit Lions.

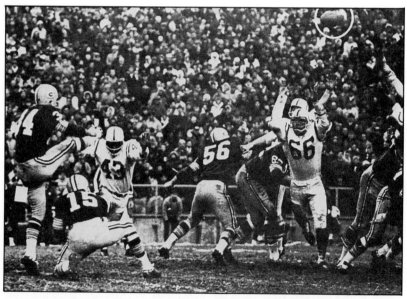

Don Chandler (34) kicks a game-winning field goal against Baltimore in 1965.

Max McGee (85) caught seven passes and scored two touchdowns against Kansas City in Super Bowl I.

Zeke Bratkowski (12) hands off to Paul Hornung (5) for a touchdown drive against Baltimore.

Hard-hitting middle linebacker
Ray Nitschke directed the
Packer defense.

Paul Hornung (5) and Fuzzy
Thurston (63) retire to the
sideline after another
successful touchdown drive.

(left to right) Paul Hornung,
Jim Taylor and Bart Starr
share the rare agony of a
Packer defeat.

In the solitude of his office,
Lombardi tries to relax.

However, on the field, Lombardi was a bundle of emotions.

The Coach frequently enjoyed
a post-game victory ride.

Lombardi holds court with the press in the Packer locker room after winning the 1966 N.F.L. Championship against Dallas.

With Frank Gifford of C.B.S. *(left)* looking on, Lombardi receives the first Super Bowl trophy from N.F.L. commissioner Pete Rozelle *(right)*.

At Lombardi's 1968 retirement
dinner, Max McGee presents
him with 5 loaves of bread and
2 fishes and then asks the
Coach to use this to feed the
5,100 in attendance.

During the 1968 season, the Washington Redskins' fans pleaded for a savior to end
the team's 13-year losing record.

Lombardi instructs Sonny Jurgensen during a Redskin preseason camp in 1969.

The Coach enjoys a moment of relaxation with his 1969 Redskin team. In one season, he turned them into winners.

studies of the upcoming opponent. Tuesday is a light workout day with exercises unknotting muscle kinks. The coaches again work late in the night making final preparations for the coming game. The offense and defense assignments are handed out Wednesday and the players go to work on them. Besides the workouts, the players view from three to four hours of films each week. By Friday, the Packers are ready to practice goal line stands. The offense busies itself with emphasizing ball control the last two minutes of each half. How to kill the clock or take advantage of it is the stress. By the time players reach the pros they are skilled in these habits, but Lombardi firmly believes the continual exercise of such play patterns comes closest to achieving perfection. Vince credits his organizational approach to football to the teachings of Earl Blaik, his head coach at Army. "Although he is a more austere man than I ever would be or could be," Vince says, "he taught me how to make my approach to a particular problem. That was the toughest thing I had to learn."

Saturday is a good day to interview Lombardi. Except for Sunday nights when Green Bay wins, he enjoys his most relaxed moments the day before the game. By then the game is largely in the hands of his team. As the Packers prepared to leave the City Stadium field after their final pre-game workout, Dominic Olejniczak, the president of the Packers and the one man Lombardi is supposedly responsible to, and Richard Bourguignon, the vice-president, explained the wonders of their stadium to me. "It seats 38,600," Bourguignon said. "We've got as many seats between the goal lines as the Los Angeles Coliseum and their capacity is 102,000. Our top row of seats, the 60th, is closer to the action than the Coliseum's first row." City Stadium is truly wonderful for fans.

As we talked, the Packers went trampling by, Lombardi among those in the rear. I had mentioned to Olejniczak that I hoped to have a few minutes with Vince before the coach went home. But something in Vince's bearing made me sense this wasn't the time. As Lombardi brushed by, Olejniczak tried to command his attention. "Not now," Vince said, "I have a meeting." He didn't say it harshly but he didn't stop walking either. I had a pretty good idea then that whatever Olejniczak's realm of influence was it didn't extend to the field. There, the Packers are led by Lombardi.

Later Vince called me into his office. His meeting was over and he was ready to sit still for an interview. I said I had found some people downtown who disliked him. To that kind of comment, the best reply that can be expected is, "So what else is new, Charley?" But Vince said, "That's my nature. I'm distant by nature. I don't think I'm unfriendly to people. I have offended some, no question about it. The job was so tremendous in the beginning." One good answer deserved more questions.

Why hadn't he taken the New York Giants' head-coaching job?

"I owe these Green Bay people something. They gave me my chance on my terms."

What are the outstanding advantages of also being general manager?

"I make my own salary arrangements with the players. I go to no one to make policy. I make it."

After the opening upset by the Lions, how would the '61 Packers do?

It's hard to keep winning. No other sport requires the self-denial or dedication to continue winning that football does. We have a good team. Baltimore has an unusually great performer in Johnny Unitas. We have tough non-conference foes. This is going to be a difficult season."

When Lombardi left his house the Sunday of the 49er game, he began it just like any other day. He went to church. As the capacity crowd, 38,669, filed into City Stadium, the Green Bay Packers began dressing. It was mostly quiet. This was almost a must-win game. There was some laughter when Henry Jordan said about a halfback teammate, "He's got more meat on his ribs than I got in my refrigerator."

"Too bad you can't be in here at the half," a veteran Packer told me. "Vince can move you like the great ones could with his halftime talks. All have their techniques. Vince does it with words. He's got a great gift. Others reach the pitch of excitement that the game has reached and can hardly get the words out. Not Lombardi. Whether the situation calls for emotion or calmness, he always seems to have the right words."

This last inkling to the Lombardi texture is contrary to many sportswriters conception of Vince. I don't know if he has ever been emotional in front of the working press. He has been in front of teams. He has been in front of friends. He softened into tears when more than 300 friends and relatives gathered at a party held for him last April upon his return to Sheepshead Bay in Brooklyn. Frank Gifford, Kyle Rote, Jack Mara, Chris Schenkel and Tom Meany made speeches that detailed Vince's glowing success and touched on the fineness of the man. When Vince rose to speak, he said, "I feel like the Irishman who beat his wife, was always drunk, a liability to the world but at his funeral the preacher told how wonderful he had been. The deceased's wife turned to one of her children and asked him to peek in the casket and make sure they were at the right funeral." Vince paused for laughter. "I can't believe you're talking about me. May I always have a good enough sense of humor to be serious, but never to take myself too seriously."

This stocky winning coach paced the Green Bay sideline as his team fought its late-September war with the 49ers. His territory is from one 40-yard line to the other. He doesn't extend beyond that very often. He smokes often and he reacts. He was pleased with his team's defensive effort that day, less than satisfied with the offense. The Packers won, 30-10, but the game was tougher than the score. On a fourth and goal situation on the San Francisco 1-yard line, with the score 23-10 in the second half, he sent in the field goal kicking team. He got booed from the stands but three cracks at the 49er line had netted only four yards. He would have liked the touchdown but the safest try was for three points. A good boot meant San Francisco would have to score three times.

Hornung missed the field goal and the crowd booed some more. A guy in the wheelchair section near the Packer bench said, "That crap belongs to New York, Lombardi. Not Green Bay." It may be a small town, but its people want a winner just like the big N.F.L. cities. Star end Max McGee was supported off the field with an ankle injury. But he returned to the game later and scored the touchdown that put the win away ("There's no room for small hurts!").

A short while after the game, we took off for Vince's home in his Pontiac. Traffic was heavy and Lombardi was still tense. He didn't like the way the cop handled the traffic. "Oh," he said relaxing as he turned the car into a less traveled road, "I played golf yesterday." He had told me he had planned to relax late Saturday by reading. He wanted to set the record straight and this conciseness is part of the man. He had shot a 91, about ten strokes above his normal game. "I swing real hard," he said, "and because I'm unorthodox I've got to hit about two dozen balls before I start out to do any good. I didn't do that yesterday." Work and play, he does both of them hard.

"Vince isn't a great golfer," said one businessman who's played with him, "but he's a great competitor. He hates to be beaten."

"He'd hate to lose in marbles," is the way Paul Hornung puts it.

Driving through the residential area, we passed many attractive homes. "Green Bay isn't a poor town," Vince said. "Almost three-quarters of the people own their own homes. This is one of the few cities in the United States that never had a depression."

Vince lives in a ranch-style home, one house removed from a river. He poured Scotches for both of us and told me I had complete freedom to look his home over for story notes. In the den there are the statuette horses won by his daughter, Susan, in riding competition. There is also a statue of the back end of a horse that was Susan's gift to Vince on Father's Day. Vince's deep laugh boomed when he showed me the gift. Framed on the wall are two pictures. Each is of a young man in football uniform with No. 40 on it. One is Vince at Fordham, the other is "Little Vince" in high school. In the house, I had a talk with Marie Lombardi. She talks more than Vince, mostly because she is filled with pride that comes from being the closest observer of his success.

"You know what Vince really wanted out of life," she said, "was to be head coach at Fordham. He didn't want it the first time when he left for West Point. There was too much unpleasantness. Anyway he needed those five years with Blaik. Blaik gave him that something extra. Vince is a teacher, then a coach. Even the year after he went to the Giants, Vince still would have gone to Fordham. He wanted to rebuild Fordham's football as it had been in the days he played there. Vince takes great pleasure in building something out of nothing. That's part of the reason why we came here. There were people at Fordham who would never have let him do it his way. He wanted to go there but looking back, we're lucky Fordham dropped football.

"It's been an even keel of success for Vince — gradual. We're old enough now that if things started to go bad, we could take it. Other coaches have had their success when they were young and then experienced the terrifying battle to retain it. We've been watched over."

Vince enjoyed himself Sunday night and Monday morning he was anxiously waiting for the film that was going to lead up to a win over the Chicago Bears. Back in New York, Reid Halahan, the old St. Cecilia player, said, "You know how people say 'nice guy' when the name of somebody they know comes up in conversation. Well, when Lombardi's name is brought up to someone who has played for him, been his student or worked with him, you don't get the usual reply. You get 'great coach' or 'great teacher' or 'great speaker.' Check me on this."

Reid called the shot. I saw Jim Lee Howell the next day.

"Lombardi?" Howell said. "Great coach."

20

A Game for Madmen
by Vince Lombardi
and W.C. Heinz

How many times the thought has come to my mind and how many times I have voiced it, I do not know, but at many a moment on many a day, I am convinced that pro football must be a game for madmen, and I must be one of them.

The Green Bay Packers may beat the Chicago Bears 49-0, as we did five years ago, but 12 hours later, I won't be enjoying the contented sleep of the victor. I will be lying there wide awake, my gums aching, because all afternoon on that sideline, I have been gnashing my teeth, and I will know that we are by no means as good a ball club as that score would indicate. The Bears came in badly depleted by injuries, and next week we've got the Detroit Lions. Am I dreaming up dragons, and is my concern just manufactured? No. Against the Lions, it takes an interception by Herb Adderly, with a minute and 40 seconds left to play, and a field goal by Paul Hornung in the last 33 seconds to beat them 9-7. That's what I mean.

I mean, too, something that happened suddenly at a practice session of last season.

We were all out on that field across Oneida Street from Lambeau Field, and suddenly I was rushing at one of my players and flailing away at him with my fists. I am 54 years old now, and he is eight inches taller than I am and outweighs me by 50 pounds. If he had brought both of his hands down on me, he probably could have driven me into the ground, but he just stood there, warding off my blows because he understands me. Fortunately, all of the Packers understand me.

What was I doing? Did I hate him, or even dislike him? No, not for a moment. I'm fond of him. He's one of the most likable men on our squad. That's his problem. He has all the size and ability he needs to be a great one, but he loves everybody. In a game, they beat on him. Everybody whacks him, and he laughs. When you criticize him, he laughs, so what was I doing? I guess I was trying to reach him in the only way left. I guess I was trying to get him to hate me enough to take it out on the opposition, because to play this game you must have that fire in you, and there is nothing that stokes that fire like hate.

I'm sorry, but that is the truth. When I served as backfield coach at West Point under Earl Blaik, I learned more from him than I have ever learned from any other man. One of the things that Blaik used to say was: "To beat the Navy, you have to hate the Navy."

What kind of game is this, then, that requires the constant conjuring of animosity? Each year, and probably more than once a year, I tell our team that, during the football season, there are only three things in which each man should be interested: 1) his family; 2) his religion; and 3) the Green Bay Packers. I coach this game, however, at no small cost to my family. I am a religious man whose religion, as all true religions, is based on love of fellowman, and yet each week, as I talk about our opponents, I almost snarl against them. Why? It is as simple as this: When Bob Jeter, our right cornerback, has to play against Baltimore's Raymond Berry, or Herb Adderly, at our other corner, is going against Detroit's Pat Studstill, day by day, the hate has to build layer upon layer, or Jeter will not have the tenacity to defeat that great sideline pattern of Berry's or Adderly to stay with that great speed and deep move of Studstill's.

"The day of a game," my wife Marie has said, "Vince hates everybody connected with that other team, but after the game — win, lose or draw — it's over."

I don't *think* that's true. I *know* it's true. Two years after I got out of Fordham University, I gave up law school so that we could be married. I took a job, coaching football and basketball and teaching Latin, chemistry and physics, at St. Cecilia High School in Englewood, N.J. One of our closest friends was Red Garrity, the basket-ball coach of the Englewood High School. We played duplicate bridge together, went to New York shows together, and celebrated birthdays, anniversaries and New Year's Eves together. During the week of the St. Cecilia-Englewood basketball game, however, we didn't even speak to each other in church.

There was fun in coaching then that I've never found since and certainly cannot find now. When I started at St. Cecilia, they paid me $1,700 a year for that teaching and coaching, and for two sum-mers, I went to Seton Hall to get masters' credits in education. For four summers, I was a road foreman of a highway-construction gang, and the truck drivers were a tough crew and the dozer and shovel men were great pros and I loved it.

Some 25 years have gone by since then, but it isn't just nostalgia that makes the difference. Will I ever be able to reminisce about the Super Bowl game as I can about the other? Hardly. The one was fun, and the Super Bowl could never be that. We in pro football had created a monster. It was the first game between the two leagues — the American Football League, which was six years old, and the Na-tional Football League, 46 years old. With the Columbia Broadcast-ing System carrying the N.F.L. games and the National Broadcast-ing Company the A.F.L., it also became a contest between the net-works. Together, they paid $2,000,000 for the television and radio rights for just this one game, and there were to be 65,000,000 people watching it on TV.

In the two weeks we had to prepare to meet the Kansas City Chiefs, every owner in our league called me on the telephone or wrote to me to try to express what this game meant. It wasn't only Packer prestige, but the whole N.F.L. was on the line. We had everything to lose and nothing to gain.

We had never seen Kansas City play, but we did exchange three game films. Even then, we could not rate them precisely because we were not familiar with their A.F.L. opposition, but going into that game, there was one thing I believed. Technically, there was no way they could beat the Green Bay Packers. If my team went out and played its kind of a football game, there was one chance in 25 of us losing, but that, too, is what makes this a game for madmen.

You live with the fear that one of your defensive backs will fall down, as Tom Brown, a good ballplayer who is going to be a better one, did against Dallas in the N.F.L. Championship. That gave them a touchdown, but luckily, it didn't cost us the game and our title. You live with the fear that your receivers will drop the ball, and too many of them have done that too often to be cited.

As it turned out, neither of these happened, and what we had seen of Kansas City in their films was the truth of them. We could see they were weak at their cornerbacks and that the stacked defenses — linebackers behind linemen and dealing to one side or the other to confuse the offensive blocking — would make them difficult to run against. At the same time, however, it would make their cornermen even more vulnerable. We saw that they liked to rotate their defenses toward the strength of the offensive formation. With that defensive alignment, the Chiefs couldn't possibly stop our passing game, so we concentrated on that and kept our running game simple.

When you win a big game like the Super Bowl by as convincing a score as 35-10, your inclination is to believe that it was played on its merits. You should be able to enjoy the rewards without detraction. There was one other statistic associated with that game, however: There were 1,306 press credentials issued, and the press can be, and often is, a horror for me.

For much of this, I take the blame. I am shy among strangers, and I guess that the sports press and I, with some exceptions, were cast to be strangers. More that that, I run scared with the press because, although I recognize the contributions it makes to the popularity of our sport, I also know how it thrives on controversy, and too many of its members have no sense of responsibility. By omission of portions of what you say, they distort what you say. The repetition of the same question altered only slightly turns an interview into a game of wits. My game is pro football, not Twenty Questions, but there I was, moments after I came off that field, mentally tired and emotionally depleted, with a microphone thrust at me, lights in my face, ringed by reporters and with millions of viewers watching on TV.

"I think they have a real fine offensive football team," I was saying, nervous and pounding that game ball in my hands. I kept talking. "I'm not going to say anything detrimental about anybody, and I'm not going to make a fool of anybody."

I should have known that wouldn't be enough. How, they wanted to know now, would Kansas City compare with Dallas? With Baltimore? I recognize those to be legitimate questions, so I gave an honest opinion, and, of course, some reporters labeled me an ungracious winner.

"That's a good football team," I said to the reporters and TV people, "but it's not as good as the top teams in our league. That's what you wanted me to say, and now I've said it. It took me a long time to get that out."

That's our game, though, this game for madmen. It arouses such violent emotions, and those emotions feed latent prejudice. In our N.F.L. Championship game, when our daughter Susan heard the epithet of "Wop!" screamed down at me, she cried.

After we lost to the Bears at Chicago in 1963, Hazel Brusky, the wife of Gene Brusky, one of our two team doctors, was crying. "But, Hazel," my wife said, "It isn't that important, it was just a game." Hazel said, "It isn't that, it's what they were saying to you in the stands."

The better and more successful we are, of course, the worse this becomes. That is the irony associated with success in this business. It doesn't make the job or your life easier. Everybody in the league is shooting at you, on the field and off, which is expected, but there is also an unexpected alteration in attitude on your own team.

When I came here in 1959, this team and this organization were in chaos. The previous year they had won one game, tied one and lost ten. When we began to win, every win was an occasion for public elation. It didn't matter how impressively we won. Since then, we have won five Western Conference titles and four N.F.L. championships, and now if we don't win big, it's almost as if we have lost, and I can feel the difference in the attitude in those stands.

After we won our first N.F.L. title, we gave each of the players' wives a mink stole. That's how important I believe wives are the success of a professional team. Some of these wives were survivors of that other era, when one day, the young daughter of Jim Ringo, who was a great center for the Packers, came home from school crying and said: "Daddy, are you a bum?" Those Packer wives knew what it was to win because they knew what it was to lose, and after they received the stoles, I was overwhelmed with letters and telephone calls expressing their thanks.

When we won again the next year, the wives had a choice of a color television set or a stereo console, and I received nice notes. For two years, we finished second, but when we won again in 1965 and sent out dinner rings, about half of the wives responded. Last year, we gave each wife a silver tea service, and I had three or four notes.

At our last stockholders' meeting, as I do each year, I presented our annual report. When I finished my first year at Green Bay as general manager and coach, we showed a net profit of $75,203. The next year, it had risen to $115,128, and each year, I have received a vote of thanks. For 1966, we showed a net profit of $827,439, and I have yet to hear that vote of appreciation.

Maybe I'm inhuman, but I am not satiated with success. Furthermore, I am not going to let this peripheral passiveness, if that is what is developing, invade my ball club. Every win for me today is still as big as that first one when, in my first head-coaching job since St. Cecilia and my first game here, we beat the Bears 9-6, and they carried me off the field.

In coaching, you speak in cliches, but I mean every one of them. There is only one yardstick in our business, and that is winning. Second place is meaningless. You can't always be first, but you have to believe that you should have been — that you are never beaten, time just runs out on you. When anyone of my ballplayers is tired of winning, or tired of paying the price winning demands, he will have a one-way ticket on a plane from Green Bay, no matter who he is.

If I am going to instill in my team this ravenous appetite for success and then maintain it against the constant threat of self-complacency, it must be deeply ingrained in me. In the eight years I coached in high school, and during the seven when I was an assistant coach at Fordham and at West Point, I wanted to be the head coach at a large university. The offers I had were from schools that were too small or from larger ones that were de-emphasizing football. I know I lost some jobs because of my Italian heritage, but whatever the reasons, the fact that I did not get the opportunities I felt I deserved motivated me greatly.

When, after I had spent five years as backfield coach with the New York Giants, I was approached about this job at Green Bay, I had one fixed idea. I insisted on being not only head coach but general manager. I had to have total responsibility. Possibly, because of the tremendous growth of professional football since I came here in 1959, the job is becoming too much for one man.

"But after the season is over," some stranger will say to me, and I can feel the hairs rising on the back of my neck, "what do you do in the off-season?" What off-season, I want to scream. I can't imagine another business that demands such complete absorption the year around.

During our training and playing season, now a six-month operation, mine is a seven-day-a-week job, and most of those are 14-16 hour days. During the rest of the year, our hours are normal, but the concentration and application are hardly less, for this is the only opportunity to eliminate some of the madness from the pro football enterprise.

Each year, following the playing season, my assistant coaches and I, for example, re-evaluate our personnel. Naturally, we don't spend much on a quarterback such as Bart Starr has become, but every player, having been rated on every play of every game, gets graded on his total performance for the season.

In our rating system, our center and guards are expected to attain at least a 60% grade in blocking on running plays, 85% on passing plays. We expect our offensive tackles to block 65% on the run, 85% on the pass, and our flankers 50% and our tight ends at least 60% on the run. They are not graded on effectiveness alone, but also on technique. There is only one way to block consistently on this team, and that is our way. Against the Colts in our opening game of last season, for example, Bob Skoronski, our left offensive tackle, blocked for 69% in 24 attempts on passes.

We rate all our receivers, of course, on pass reception. Last season, our tight end, Marv Fleming, in 52 attempts had 38 completions for 73% and 454 yards. He scored two touchdowns, averaged 8.7 yards per attempt and 12 yards per completion, and had six drops. He ran his 278 pass routes correctly 92% of the time, made 251 blocks for 74% and had no interceptions against him.

In grading our defensive men on each play of each game, we use 0 for satisfactory, 1 is better and 2 is awarded for an exceptional play such as an interception or tackling the passer. Ron Kostelnik, our left defensive tackle, participated in 848 plays and had a total of plus

13. Henry Jordan, our right defensive tackle, was in 867 plays and had a total of plus 41. Willie Davis, at left end, was 859 for plus 47.

The position played, however, has much to do with the grading. Linebackers, for example, particularly middle linebackers, have a more complicated job and most of them end up the year with a minus grade. Ray Nitschke, our middle linebacker, was in 870 plays for a minus 20; Lee Roy Caffey, our right linebacker, was 847 for minus 21; and Dave Robinson was 858 for plus 3, a truly remarkable year. Among our defensive backs, Willie Wood was 876 for plus 27; Tom Brown was 878 for plus 6; Herb Adderly was 893 for plus 12.

We also, in recording every play we run during the season, keep a record of the number of times we used each play, the number of yards it gained, the average gain and the longest gain.

We record the time, in minutes and seconds, that we are on offense and defense in each quarter of each game to prove ball control. We have reels on our wham plays, our give plays, our reverses and our sweeps. We do the same with our passing, making a composite reel of each pass against all of the defenses that each team uses. There are now 470 reels in our film library.

We are also computerized and have data processing. Each team we play is broken down on IBM cards so that we can tell instantly the number of times they used certain plays from certain formations in certain situations, and the results are recorded. We can also determine immediately their defensive preference against our formations in specific situations and what the outcome was.

The steak and potatoes of any professional football operations, though, is its talent program. To increase efficiency and cut down the expense of scouting, N.F.L. teams during the last several years have formed into three groups. The Packers share a talent-scouting operation with the Browns, the Colts, the Cardinals, the Falcons, the Giants and the Redskins, but the manhunt still costs our club over $100,000 a year and a lot of sleep.

With 26 professional teams drafting college players now, you don't dare make a mistake and waste a choice in those early rounds. With more than 80 people scouting for our group last autumn, the Packers rated highest three college seniors — Bubba Smith, the Michigan State defensive lineman; Gene Washington, the Michigan State end; and Ray McDonald, the Idaho fullback — and the Bob

Hyland of Boston College, whom we assessed as the best college offensive lineman in the country. When it came our time to pick, Smith and Washington had been taken, and we were faced with our first problem.

"All right," I said to my assistant coaches, "what do we do now?"

We draft by telephone. We sit, with two secretaries, in our conference room in Green Bay, with Ed Franco, who played with me at Fordham, on the other end of the line at the draft meeting in New York.

"Our number one need," I said, and we had some 30 separate scouting reports on Bob Hyland, "is for an offensive lineman."

"But if we don't take that McDonald," somebody said, "and the Bears do, we'll have to play against him for ten years." We took Hyland, and the Bears did not take McDonald. He went to the Redskins. Thanks to the computer and data-processing people, we can put, for example, our finger at any moment on any college flanker in the country who is over 6-feet-3 and can run the hundred in ten seconds flat. But there are human qualities that you can't program and that you can't detect until you test for them.

When a boy with all the desire and dedication and courage for which you could ask isn't quite big enough or quite quick enough, it breaks your heart. As the years have gone on, I have found that I can't take it, and Pat Peppler, our director of personnel, does most of the telling. When it comes to trading or cutting a veteran, it is even worse, and I must do it. I think the day last February when I had to call Paul Hornung in Louisville, Ky., and tell him he was no longer a Packer was the saddest day I have known in Green Bay, and there were tears at both ends of that telephone connection. There will never be another No. 5 on the Packers.

We gave up Hornung because there was no way out of it. When the New Orleans Saints were granted an N.F.L. franchise, every team but Atlanta had to make available 11 men from which the Saints could select three. Hornung was on our list because of a pinched nerve in his neck that could cause paralysis of his left side. He had played very little for us, and neither he nor I thought the Saints would pick him. It was a risk that, for the good of the club, I had to take, and he understood. Five months later, Hornung retired from pro football on doctor's orders.

When I first came to Green Bay, and after months of studying movies of all the Packer games, I knew that Paul Hornung was one of the ballplayers I really needed, although he was better known for his exploits off the field than on. With people I could take into my confidence, I investigated his reputation, and while I found that much of it was true, there was much that was exaggerated.

What I liked about Hornung, right from our first meeting, was that he never tried to deny any of the truths, and he looked me right in the eye. One year in training camp, he and Max McGee, our split end and Hornung's roommate and buddy, went out after curfew, and I fined them $500 each. There was no whimper from Hornung, or McGee, either. In 1964, on the evening before our game with the Bears in Chicago, I walked into the Red Carpet Hotel for dinner and found Hornung and his date at the bar. We have a rule on the Packers that if our players are going to imbibe in a public place, they must do it with moderation and at a table, and never on the eve of a game. When I saw Hornung at that bar, the safety valve blew, and I shouted him out of the restaurant. The next morning, when I fined him $500 again, he never even mentioned that all he was drinking was ginger ale. I know it was ginger ale because, after he left, I tasted it.

About Hornung the ballplayer, there was much I liked. He had no real speed but he was a fine runner. Inside the opponent's 20-yard line, he was a great one. He could smell that goal line. He was a good field-goal and extra-point kicker, a great blocker, but more than that, his quality of leadership was the greatest I have ever seen in a ballplayer.

Paul Hornung was the epitome of what you try to make every one of your players — a true believer. If we were going to play Detroit, and he knew I was worried, he'd say: "Coach, what are you worried about? We've got this game in the bag." He'd tell our team: "Look, there's no better prepared team in the N.F.L. than we are. We can't lose."

He made a point of being friendly to our first-year men. Elijah Pitts, who was to replace Hornung, tells how, in his rookie year, he was lying on his cot, lonely and homesick and worried, when Hornung came in and invited him to a get-together with some of the veterans. When Hornung accepted a speaking engagement, he would take one of the first-year men with him and split the fee.

Going into that Super Bowl, I was faced with a great conflict within myself. After all, it was the first Super Bowl, and Hornung, with the great years and great performances he had contributed to the Packers, deserved as much as anyone the honor of playing in it. A jamming blow on his head, however, would give him excruciating pain. In our game films, I had seen too many pictures of Hornung flinching on a block. This wasn't from lack of courage; Hornung possesses all the courage any ballplayer needs. It was a natural protective reflex, but I couldn't stomach it, and I don't think Hornung could either.

I had the thought that, if things went badly for us early in that game, if we did not dominate it as we should, I might have to use Hornung to give us that lift. As it turned out, things went well, and when, late in the game, I asked Hornung if he wanted to go in, he said, "No, Coach, it's all over."

One of the other things I always appreciated about Hornung was that although during his great years he could have held me up in salary discussions more than any other of our ballplayers, he never did. In 1961, he was voted the N.F.L.'s outstanding player; and three times, he led the league in scoring — once setting an all-time record — but we were never more than $5,000 apart in another phase of this game that can ready you for a straitjacket.

Next to releasing players, signing them is the most unpleasant part of this job. It is the only time when you and the player are not striving for the same thing, and it is not helped by the player's wife who, out of whatever need she may have, tells other player-wives that her husband is getting $20,000. It is not made easier by the player who, badly advised, walks in demanding $30,000 more than I believe he is worth, or by the one with the ultimatum pay him what he wants or trade him. They both get hustled out of my office in a hurry; and the one with the ultimatum, if he does not relent, gets traded.

I have lost two fine ballplayers because of the ultimatum — Jim Ringo, before the 1964 season, to the Philadelphia Eagles, and Jimmy Taylor this year to the New Orleans Saints. Taylor had been a great fullback for us, strong, quick off that snap, quick to spot the daylight and a great personal competitor who fought with that second effort for that extra yardage. One year, in fact, he wanted to be paid according to the yardage he gained, until I made clear to him some of the complications, including the fact that on our ball club a fullback earns his pay by blocking too. This year, when, in effect, he demanded an annuity, there was no way I could grant it and be honest with the others.

In salary negotiation, there is no place for deception. You must be completely honest, and my ballplayers know that on our ball club, a man gets paid for the job he does, and that those who play the same level of ball get the same money. The Packers' player payroll is the highest in the league, which is as it should be, and I will never cut a player's salary. To do so is to say that he not only had a bad season the year before, but that you expect him to have another one, and that is no way to restore or preserve the pride that a player must have in himself.

I don't think there are any geniuses in coaching. I believe that if you were to put all the coaches in professional football in the same room and give them all the same questions — how to defeat the 4-3, the 5-1, the zone, the man-to-man — you would get the same answers. The difference in coaches is not so much in their knowledge, but in how they organize it and communicate it.

The organization of what you know about the playing of this game and of how your opponents play it must be so complete that you and your team must know what you are doing and why you are doing it every minute that you spend on that practice field and in team meetings. Confusion scrambles the lines of communication. I may be trying to inspire a linebacker to be more aggressive, only to find that he is reluctant against the run because he is confused on pass coverage.

Inside of me as a coach, there is a switchboard that provides a line of communication to each of my players. Each line must be soldered firmly at both terminals with understanding. I am not a believer in subjecting players to I.Q. tests, and I notice that the coaches who use such instruments will play the legs off a dumb player if he's a good one. A mouse can be taught to run the right routes if you give him the proper motivation. That, though, is the maddening struggle — to try to understand the varied natures of 40 players as different, say, as Bart Starr from Ray Nitschke or Willie Davis from Marv

Fleming so that you can, by various methods, give each of them the motivation to become the player he should be to make the Green Bay Packers the team they had better be.

21

Secrets of Winning Football
by Vince Lombardi
and W.C. Heinz

The game of pro football, when compared with any science, is a simple one. It must be kept that way, because as a coach, you are not dealing neccessarily with the finest minds to come out of our colleges, although some players do have fine minds, only with the finest football players. It is the approach and the understanding of these men that is so complex.

For six months of each year, you must deal daily with 40 individuals, and your effort must be to motivate each of them equally toward the same ideal. Their flaws as football players are obvious; hidden are the reasons why they are not overcoming these flaws and fulfilling their potentials.

"I will try," I promise the new men when I talk to them as a group for the first time, "to make of each of you the best football player he can possibly be. I will try with every fiber in me, and I will try and try and try."

Every coach's team is an extension of himself, and so the personality of the coach becomes the personality of his team. I have known careless and slipshod coaches, and their teams played sloppy ball. I have known coaches who, as players, were dirty players, and their teams played dirty ball. On the other hand, Don Shula, when he was a defensive back in the National Football League, played clean, hard-nosed ball and would take the gamble. His Baltimore Colts today play clean, hard-nosed ball and will gamble. I am highly emotional, but I am also highly disciplined, and I do things according to the book, and I am conservative. My team is highly emotional, but it is controlled emotion, released for a purpose. The Packers show that discipline, and will gamble only when they must.

The player who, more than any other, must become an extension of yourself is, of course, your quarterback. When I started with the Green Bay Packers in 1959, Bart Starr was one of three quarterbacks, and the opinion on the ball club and around the league was that he would never make it. They said that he didn't throw well enough, that he wasn't tough enough and that, because he lacked confidence in himself, the team would never have confidence in him. When I studied the Packer game films, I came to the conclusion that Starr did have the ability — the arm and the ball-handling techniques. When I met him, I found that he also has a fine analytic mind and a retentive memory, but at the same time, I found him so polite and so self-effacing that I wondered if he wasn't too nice a young man to be the authoritarian leader your quarterback must be. The basic problem, though, was to instill in him that confidence in himself and in his arm, and we worked on that together for years.

"Look," I would tell him over and over, "you don't have to feel you're carrying the whole burden of this ball club. This is a good team, and when it makes mistakes, it will recover. It will perform, but if it doesn't, it won't all be your fault."

However, when a man is as intelligent and as sincere a team player as is Bart Starr, he tends to be a worrier. When he makes a costly mistake, he tends to harbor it. No one hates his own mistakes more than I, or takes his losses harder than I, but when they are over, they are over. I tell my team that mistakes are the lessons by which we learn, but once the lesson is learned, the mistake must be forgotten. Starr knows this now, and he says that one play in one game taught him his lesson.

It was in our 1964 game in Green Bay against the Colts, and with less than a minute to go, it was our ball, but they were leading us, 21-20. I sent in a pass play — a turn-in to Max McGee, our split end — that, I am still as certain as you can be about anything in this game of uncertainties, should have positioned us to kick the field goal. Starr let McGee talk him into changing the play to a turnout, and Colt cornerback Don Shinnick intercepted.

"I've made mistakes since," Starr says now, "but that was such a crucial one — it got the Colts on the right road for the rest of the season and literally wrecked us that year — that when I survived it, I knew I'd never let another mistake crush me again."

Starr worked on his weaknesses — the long ball and his lack of decisiveness — until they became his strengths. He used to throw a better turn-in to the left than to the right, but working against our Herb Adderly in practice, he rectified that. To the left, he used to pull the string a little, but against our Bob Jeter, who recovers very quickly, he learned to throw on a better string. Today, he operates out there like a surgeon. He is a master at picking those defenses apart; and three times, he has been the N.F.L.'s leading passer, and last year, he was also voted its Most Valuable Player.

When you are coaching a player with the intelligence and complete dedication of Bart Starr, it seems monstrous that you should ever have to raise your voice to him in anger, and in front of the squad. I have done it, however, and more than once.

Like my father before me, I have a violent temper with which I have been struggling all my life, and with which I have had to effect a compromise. It is ineradicable, but it must not be irrational. I coach with everything that is within me, and I employ that temper for a purpose.

The Packers came to understand this early in our relationship, and they came to understand that when I berate a man, there is nothing personal about it. I am berating a ballplayer, for his own benefit and ours, and I never carry a grudge.

In 1959, that first year in Green Bay, our rookies, as always, came in to training camp three days ahead of the squad. With them were a half-dozen veterans who did not have to be there but who, once there, were expected to abide by the regulations. One night, two of those veterans took off, and I did not see them again until three mornings later, when I collared them in the hall and, they say, grabbed one of them by his lapels and started to bang his head against the wall. They say you could hear me all over that dormitory and that, after it was over, the one I jumped said: "I'm not gonna play for this. . . . He's a madman!"

An hour later, I was leaving the dormitory to walk across campus to a squad meeting when I caught up with the man. I slapped him on the back and said: "C'mon, Max, let's get to this meeting."

I had forgotten the whole incident, and the man was Max McGee, who was a fine receiver when I came with this club and who has been a fine one since. This past season, he made a key catch against the Colts in a game that meant the Western Conference title; he caught the last touchdown against Dallas for the N.F.L. title; and grabbed seven passes, including two for touchdowns, in the Super Bowl against Kansas City.

Sometimes, you will make a man, such as Bart Starr, a target in front of the team not because he needs it, and in that manner, but to impress someone else who can't take public criticism. When I call Henry Jordan, our right defensive tackle, or Lionel Aldridge, our right defensive end, in front of the club, however, it is because they do need it. They are both intelligent ballplayers — Jordan, for many years an All-Pro, and Aldridge, developing into one — but they tend to be satisfied, and they need the whip, and they know it.

"I'll say one thing for the Coach," Jordan has often been quoted, "he treats us all the same — like dogs."

For years, Ray Nitschke, our middle linebacker, has been the rowdy of the ball club and the number-one whipping boy, but happily, marriage settled him down and did things for him that, I guess, criticism never could. Nitschke is big, rough and belligerent, but he is also a fun-loving guy with a heart as big as our Lambeau Field. When I would chew him out, he would be like a child — repentant, and never giving you an argument — but then he'd turn around and do the same thing over again. Criticism still rolls off him until I wonder if it helps, but he improves himself.

The most improved member of our ball club last season was Marv Fleming, our big tight end, and another one I have blown my top at again and again. When I see now the ballplayer that Fleming is finally becoming after four years, I realize that surely this must be a game for madmen, because with Fleming, I almost missed.

Time after time, I would have his bag packed, and then I would look at his size and strength and speed, and I would resolve that there had to be some way to reach him. He lacked agility, so we brought in a rope and had him skip it. But his big problem was one of concentration. He would blow assignments almost every time we used him, even in practice, until finally we convinced him that it takes mental as well as physical dedication to play this game.

Players make players, too, because they are severe critics. They would look at the size and ability of that Fleming, and for awhile, they were disgusted with him. I think this affected him, but he's a smiler who gets serious when you criticize him, and success on a ball club breeds liking. On the fourth play of our game against the Detroit Lions last season, he took a short pass over the middle and broke a tackle and went 53 yards for a touchdown. In the fourth period against Dallas, in the N.F.L. Championship game, with a third and 19 on our 43-yard line, he took the ball away from two linebackers and caught one for 24 yards when we really needed it. As he has improved, his popularity has grown.

Another ballplayer I almost missed on is Herb Adderly. As a fine offensive back at Michigan State, he was our first-round draft choice for 1961, and Bill Austin, who was our offensive line coach then and is now head coach of the Pittsburgh Steelers, signed him on the hood of a car in a parking lot in San Francisco after swapping punches with a coach from the Canadian League who apparently wanted Adderly as much as we did.

All through training camp and into the season, I tried to incorporate Adderly into our offense. I decided to use his speed and open-field ability by making a flanker out of him. When we found out he has great hands and was a natural at running those pass routes, I thought we had it made, but when we put him into a game, nothing happened. He just didn't look like the same ball player, and because I could never get him to loosen up and talk freely with me, I put Emlen Tunnell, who was then a defensive back with us and a great clubhouse information man, on him.

"I'll tell you what's bothering Adderly," Emlen said a couple of days later. "He doesn't want to be a flanker. He wants to be a defensive back."

I had been so stubborn that I had been trying the impossible — to make something of a man that he didn't want to be. Adderly, of course, has become one of the great defensive backs and an annual All-Pro.

A year earlier, at the draft meeting in Philadelphia, the other clubs had thought I was kidding when, for our thirteenth choice, I announced: "The Packers draft Elijah Pitts of Philander Smith." We didn't have great expectations for Elijah, and his first couple of years here, we considered him just a stopgap that we hoped we could replace. Here, again, I was lucky, because some ballplayers mature slowly and late, and Elijah was one of them.

We indoctrinated him, as we do all our rookies, on our kicking and receiving teams, and he became one of our best special-team members. His confidence grew. He always had good speed, we found that he had good hands, and he developed physically.

"Hey!" we coaches would hear ourselves saying, watching our game films. "Look at Pitts! He never goes down with the first tackle."

The job of picking up the slack for an injured Paul Hornung became Elijah's, and he grew into it. It frightens you, though, when you think how, in spite of the never-ending effort you make to understand and evaluate every ballplayer you draft and coach, you can almost miss on some and actually miss on others.

My first year here, I had, as a rookie, Tim Brown. He was a good-looking back, with great speed and quickness, but we had five other running backs and were carrying him into the first week of the seaons, but then he dropped a punt against the Bears in our first league game, and my first as a head coach, and the next day, I let him go. With Philadelphia, he has been a great back, and he has set N.F.L. records for most yards gained in a single game and in a season.

When we keep a ballplayer, he not only has an obligation to the Packers but we have an obligation to him. No ballplayer must ever stop trying out for this team, no matter how long he has been a member, and we must never stop trying to make him better.

Bob Long is a flanker who will be going into his fourth season with us, and he has three problems. He has great speed and great moves, but he catches too many passes out-of-bounds. He has to learn to feel those sidelines the way Raymond Berry of the Colts does. He also must recognize those defenses more quickly. Beyond this, Long worries too much about the unusual, while the old pros know that the unusual is just a one- or two-shot thing.

All of this comes with experience, and at the University of Wichita, where he was a fine basketball player, Long played only one year of football. When he was a rookie here, I sent him into a preseason game against the Giants, and he dropped a pass in the open. I remember that when he came off the field, I threw my arm around his shoulders because there were tears in his eyes. This may be the year when he overcomes that lack of experience and becomes a fine one.

They all have their problems, which become my problems. What I have said about Bart Starr — an intelligent and sincere man with that worrying tendency — I can say about the best among them. No coach could ask for a more sincere ballplayer, for example, than Willie Davis, our left defensive end and defensive captain, and another regular All-Pro.

Willie grew up in Arkansas and was the oldest of three children. His parents separated when he was young, and his mother worked in a country club where Willie was a locker-room boy during vacations. He played for Grambling College, and you never have to talk to Willie about dedication.

"Pro football," he says, "has been the difference between me being just another guy and having something today. I was from just a small Negro school, and I sometimes shake when I think that I might not have finished college and not made a pro club."

Willie never leaves pro football. Between games, and even between seasons, he replays game situations over and over in his mind, analyzing his errors. Of course, he's a worrier — not worried about the team winning, but worried about how Willie Davis will play. Like many ballplayers, he doesn't eat much the morning of a game; but often, he can't eat until the day after a game, so I always have to try to keep him loose going in.

"I try to play," he says, and it would be hard to improve on this, "so I can live with myself."

Bob Skoronski, our left tackle and offensive captain, is so high-strung that enormous emotional pressure builds up inside him before a game. Before Norm Masters retired, I used to alternate Skoronski and Masters at left tackle. I learned that if I did not start Skoronski, he would undergo some sort of psychological relapse and not play up to his talent, and last year, he had his best year.

Dave Robinson, our left linebacker, is a worrier, but he is also the complete football player. He was our first-draft choice for 1963 out of Penn State, where he was just about everybody's all-America. He delights, as you must on defense, in hitting people out there, and he has that other talent that all the great ones have, the knack of making the big play.

He has done it repeatedly, but never with more in the balance than in our N.F.L. Championship game against Dallas last season. If we did not win, we would not represent the N.F.L. against the Kansas City Chiefs in the first Super Bowl. All that we had built and accomplished at Green Bay in eight years would be dwarfed. It came down to one play.

With a minute and 14 seconds remaining, we were ahead, 34-27, but they had the ball, fourth down on our two-yard line. If they scored, we would go into sudden-death overtime. Dallas went into left formation, away from the near sideline, with Bob Hayes, their fine receiver, at tight right end. Don Meredith faked to two backs and then bootlegged to his right on the option run-pass they call "fire 90 quarterback roll right." Leon Donohue, their right guard, pulled, but Robinson sliced in behind him, fought to the outside, pushed off a blocker, threw up his hands to screen Meredith's receivers and then grabbed Don. Meredith barely got the ball away, and Tom Brown intercepted in the end zone.

Ironically, on the most important play of the season, and although Robinson saved us on it, when we rated him on it, as we rate every player on every play, we had to mark him low. The proper technique called for Robinson to make his charge to the outside to force Meredith to stop his rollout. Robinson said:

"I tried to pin both his arms, but all I could get was his left. As I grabbed him, I thought that I hadn't done what I was supposed to do. Under Coach Lombardi, you always try for perfection, and if I had played this perfectly, I would have had both of his arms."

Dave is an engineering graduate, and he has that kind of a mind. We tell all of our players not only what to do, but why they must do it that way. Some of them are only obedient; they don't care why. Robinson always has to know the reason why, and if he doesn't know it, he asks, and you can't get out of the meeting. A man whose mind explores not only all the reasons but all the implications is going to be a worrier. That is a definite weakness, and I must work not against that fine mind but with it, to alleviate the worry.

"When Vin gets one he thinks can be a real good ballplayer," my wife has said, "I feel sorry for that boy. Vin will just open a hole in that boy's head and pour everything he knows into it, and there's no way out of it. I don't want to watch it."

I think that a boy with talent has a moral obligation to fulfill it, and I will not relent on my own responsibility. Talent is not only a blessing, it is a burden, as the gifted ones we get soon find out.

Two of the gifted ones in whom we have a lot at stake are Donny Anderson and Jim Grabowski. They were both first-round draft choices, and it is no secret that I hope to make of them the Paul Hornung and Jim Taylor of the future. They were both great college players, both consensus all-America for two years — Anderson as a halfback at Texas Tech, and Grabowski as a fullback at Illinois, where he broke Red Grange's records and six conference marks.

Anderson has that big racehorse stride that eats up ground, and he has the elusiveness; but last season, he was running away from his interference. We also have to teach him to button up as he meets a tackler, to get that extra yardage and to protect himself. This is not easy to teach those who have a natural upright style of running.

Grabowski has that short, choppy stride you want in your fullback, with more speed than most, and he's tremendously quick. But he must learn to spot that hole quickly and go to that daylight, and it takes time before this becomes almost instinctive.

Last season, with Jimmy Taylor and Elijah Pitts carrying the load, and Paul Hornung available in spots, I was able to brake Anderson and Grabowski into this game gradually.

All real football players, though, are straining at the leash to play regularly. One day, I spoke to both of them, "Someday," I said, "you're going to thank me for not throwing you right in there."

"I already thank you," Anderson answered for both.

Will they, and the other young ones we're depending on, give me all they've got? I think so, but you never know until week after week, for 14 games, the going gets tougher and tougher and tougher.

Football people are a breed of their own. You don't ask a salesman to go to work with a sprained ankle, and we don't ask anyone to risk permanent injury. Bart Starr and Max McGee, however, have played with cracked ribs; Paul Hornung, with that pinched nerve in his neck; Boyd Dowler, with a painful calcification of the shoulder;

Ken Bowman, with a dislocated shoulder that they would put back into place in the dressing room; Fuzzy Thurston, with an ankle the size of his calf.

Many great athletes, however, are front-runners. There have been outstanding players, who, when things got bad, ran for cover; and then I've got Forrest Gregg, at our offensive right tackle, who, if the score was 50-0 against us, would still be out there trying to kill somebody.

In the effort to understand your players better, you want to get as close to them as you can, but unlike some coaches, I constantly repress the urge to fraternize. I do not believe that you gain their confidence by being one of them. I hold it to be more important to have the players' confidence than their affection.

The strength of the group is in the strength of the leader. As someone has said, "Confidence is contagious, and so is lack of confidence." Many a morning, when I am worried or depressed, I have to give myself what is almost a pep talk, because I am not going before that ball club without being able to exude assurance. I must be the first believer, because there is no way in which you can hoodwink the players as to confidence. They read their coach too well. By the time we go into any game, I must be convinced that we are as well-prepared as we can possibly be, that we will play as well as we are capable of playing, and maybe even better.

Although your confidence grows in proportion to the degree of your preparation, there is one danger in being well-prepared. You tend to stay with what you have decided to do, rather than adapt, and a classic example of this was our Thanksgiving Day game in Detroit in 1962, when millions on national TV saw us take a really bad beating.

For that game, the Lions came up with a surprise defense. In the first half, they were all over Bart Starr, dropping him eight times for minus 76 yards, recovering a fumble for a touchdown and tackling him for a safety. It was chaos, thanks to coaching stupidity. Not until the second half did we change our tactics. By then, we were behind 23-0, and they beat us 26-14. It was the only game we lost that year.

We have our weaknesses, of course, as individuals and as a team. We don't do the job we should covering and receiving kicks. Our kicks go too far or not far enough or to the wrong place, and we haven't spent enough time on that tactic. We don't break our runners for long gains, only partially because we haven't had that type of runner, and we have a psychological weakness too. Going into a game, we are so high that we drain quickly. When we get ahead by a couple of touchdowns, as we did against Dallas in the last N.F.L. Championship, the wind seems to go out of us, and we play satisfied and conservative ball. I am not interested in running up scores — but when you don't maintain your momentum, you can end up, as happened to us against Dallas, fighting for your life.

Most professional teams have a tendency to slack off on fundamentals. When you coach in college, you don't have this problem because you are getting new people all the time. But when you are dealing with professionals, you have the feeling that they have been here for seven or eight years and that they should know how to block and tackle. They do, but they don't want to persist on fundamentals because they're bored. It is old hat to them and to us.

This is a game of pride, and we always took particular pride in protecting our quarterback. People marveled; and then the opposition started to get to Bart Starr. At first, we thought that perhaps he was not getting back far enough. He is a quick and rhythmic passer. He takes those three steps back and cocks his arm, and that takes 1.5 seconds. In less than a second, he makes his throw. But once in a while, he has to hold for a fraction of a second more, and we discovered that in those cases, he would almost invariably get caught.

Our linemen were unconsciously blocking only for the time it normally took Starr to unload, and then they would turn around with their mouths open to see him go down.

For our practice sessions, we had a local jeweler rig up a stop clock, with a buzzer on it set to go off at three seconds, even when the pass has already been completed.

Boredom is a constant enemy. In training camp, we give our offense, as quickly as we can, those 40 plays that are going to constitute our basic attack, and in the next six months, they are going to run them over and over. Teams do not go physically flat, but they go mentally stale. Each week of the playing season, we will incoporate four or five additional things, designed especially for the opponent. But as the season goes on, and to combat staleness, I will save a special play for Saturday. It will have some unusual quality, to challenge the players and pick them up.

For some time, I had planned the first play we used against Dallas in the N.F.L. Championship. We had known it would be good against the Cowboys, but I kept it from the players until Saturday. I was not afraid we would be mentally stale or emotionally flat for a game of such importance, but I knew my team had come to expect that something a little special at the last moment. We knew that Dallas, against our Red formation, used a staggered defense in which they keyed their middle linebacker on our fullback, who normally went to the side of the play. What we did was send Jimmy Taylor away from the play and bring Elijah Pitts back in the opposite direction, which required some blocking changes for our right guard and right tackle and a trap on their left end. Pitts went 32 yards before Mel Renfro, one of the fastest men in the league, pulled him down, and we took it in from there.

What every coach tries to do, of course, is find a definite weakness in the opponent and milk it. We particularly try to find a weakness in a strong area. When we succeed there, we are not only exploiting a flaw, but we are also, by hurting the opponent in what he has held to be his strength, rocking his confidence.

Gino Marchetti of the Baltimore Colts was one of the great defensive ends. He was strong and agile, a tremendous pass rusher, with such great strength in his arms that he would just spin those pass blockers by the shoulders if they let him get his hands on them. He would play on the outside shoulder of your tackle, and as the tackle blocked down, he'd close, looking for the play on the inside. What we were able to do now and then against Marchetti was block our tackle down on the defensive tackle and then run outside. When we did, you could see that whole Baltimore team looking as if they couldn't believe it.

It all comes down to this: In a football game, there are approximately 150 plays. We play a 14-game schedule, so there are, more or less, about 2,000 plays. If I am going to get out of my team, made up of men of varied talents and varied temperaments, the utmost effort by each man on each play, I must sell each one this truth: our studies show that the difference between the winning and the losing of a game hinges, on the average, on a minimum of two plays and a maximum of five; and of course, at any time, at any place on the field, it may hinge on one. Each man must go all out on every play because no one knows when that big play is coming up.

Is it any wonder I have called this a game for madmen and admit to being one of them?

22

I Miss the Fire
on Sunday
by W.C. Heinz

"Right now," he had said, "I miss it fiercely. First of all, I miss the rapport with the players. I was close to them, and they to me. Today I feel as if I'm nothing to them. When I meet one of them he says: 'Hello, Mister Lombardi.' And that's it.

"I don't miss the week, though. I don't miss the meetings and the practices. I'd get up at 6 a.m. and come home at 5:30 for dinner. Then I'd start to watch the news on TV and my head would nod and I'd get up and go to work again, at the meeting from 7 to 10 or 11.

"I don't miss any of that," he had said, "but what I miss is the fire on Sunday."

It was 10:10 a.m. now and a Sunday, and the Green Bay Packers would be playing the Philadelphia Eagles. It was the first Sunday of the National Football League season, and Vince Lombardi, once more on his way to the stadium, had driven down the elm-lined avenue that leads into DePere, Wis., and then over the bridge across the Fox River. In 1959 Vince Lombardi, as head coach and general manager, had taken the Green Bay Packers, the worst team in the N.F.L., and in three years he had made them the best. In his nine years they had won five N.F.L. titles, three in a row, and the two Super Bowl games played up to now. Then, in February of this year, he had turned over the head-coaching job to Phil Bengtson, to remain as general manager.

"Nobody," his wife Marie had said, "will ever know the kind of pressure it was. It's too much to ask anybody to do, year in and year out. Every now and then he'd say: 'I'm going to quit.' And I'd say: 'Oh, yes?'

"Then a year ago I knew it. He would come home, during the times when they were in a slump, and he'd get in that big chair and be so mentally and physically beaten. He'd say: 'What's the matter with the world today? What's the matter with people? I have to go on that field every day and whip people. It's for them, not just me, and I'm getting to be an animal.' "

He was driving north on Highway 41, the sun glaring off the concrete and off the hood of the car. In the old days, the days as old as a year ago, he would be settling on the opening offensive play. It would be a play designed to impress, as in the time when Joe Schmidt, who is now the head coach of the Detroit Lions, was the best middle linebacker in the business, and Vince Lombardi opened against Detroit with Brown Right 73. First, Jim Ringo and then Ron Kramer hit Schmidt, and finally Bob Skoronski caught Schmidt reeling and flattened him, with his feet up in the air, five yards from the line of scrimmage. For the next half dozen plays Joe Schmidt was all eyes, and the Lions were impressed.

"We'll have a million things go wrong today," Vince Lombardi was saying now. "Ticket takers. Ushers. Police. Lost tickets." He drove across the almost empty expanse of the paved parking area to the offices he had built at the north end of the stadium on what was Highland Avenue before they changed it to Lombardi Avenue last August 7.

"When training camp opened this year," he said, and he was sorting through the papers on the big walnut desk in his office on the second floor, "I had to force myself to stay away. I went out and had dinner there that first night and then on and off, and I had breakfast out there every morning, but it was a great effort not to be a real part of it.

"One thing you can be sure of," he said. "I'm not going to interfere on that field this year. There's absolutely no way I'm going to be a part of it on that field."

He walked to the window and looked down at the parking area. The people were getting out of their cars and starting to set up the card tables, the lounge chairs and bring out the beer.

"Look at that guy!" he said."He's bringing out a charcoal burner! There's a guy with a lawn chair! All these years, and I've never noticed this before!"

It was 11 o'clock, and he went down and started on his tour of the stadium with Tom Miller, his assistant.

"That's good," he was saying, walking along under the concrete stands, the people coming in turning to look at him and then to whisper to one another. "We've got that blocked off there now, and they can't get in over there."

He was talking about barbed wire. There had been gaps in the wire atop the eight-foot chain-link fence that surrounds the stadium and they had estimated that at every game about 2,000 crashers had come through.

"This is real bad here," he was saying now, referring to a van selling cotton candy and parked too close to one of the gates. "In an emergency the people couldn't get out of this gate."

"Right," Tom Miller said, making a note in a small black notebook.

And you see what should be done here?" he was saying, stopping at one of the green-painted wooden concession stands. "They should paint that concrete behind there green, too."

It was 11:14 a.m., and in the old days, a year ago, he would have been in the coaches' office, which was off the locker room. He would have had one of those 8x11 cards in his hands — the ready list — weighing once more those offensive plays from left formation on one side of the card and those from right formation on the other.

Now it was barbed wire and cotton candy and green paint, and all week it had been the general manager's job. It hadn't been the practice field and the team meetings and the game films over and over, but instead the meetings with the police and the first aid people and the head ushers and ticket takers and concessionaires. On Tuesday, he had flown to New York for two days of league meetings. Then there had been the negotiations over Packer player contracts and the negotiations for a preseason game in 1970 and a meeting on Packer tax problems. There had been talks about replacing the stadium sod with synthetic turf, and there were always the telephone calls and the mail.

"I guess," he had said, one of those days, "that the reason I gave up the coaching was that with all the new problems — with the Packer organization growing and with the league problems becoming more complicated — and with Phil available, I could make a greater contribution in the front office.

"I thought of continuing and getting rid of some of the duties, but I'm not made that way. I had to dig everything out of the game pictures. I wouldn't let anybody else do it. I wouldn't let anybody else talk to the quarterbacks. I had to drive everybody — my players, my family and myself.

"As we kept winning, the press used to ask me: 'What else can you accomplish?' You never become satisfied with winning. Every time you put a team on the field you think: Suppose nobody ever saw my team before? Every time the team makes a mistake it's your mistake, and there are 60,000,000 people watching on TV."

He had finished now the tour of the stadium, and as he came into the hallway outside the dressing rooms he saw Joe Kuharich, the head coach of the Eagles.

"Joe," he said, and they shook hands, "how are you?"

"I'm all right," Kuharich said, "but what about you? You ready to start all over again?"

"No."

"You'll be back," Kuharich said. "I know. I was out for a year. You're only 54."

"Anyway," he said, "good to see you."

He walked through the green-carpeted Packer dressing room, through the confusion of players dressing. He once said that a quarterback must be an extension of his coach, and now he was shaking hands with Bart Starr, whom he made into the most precise and efficient quarterback in the game.

"So have a good game and a good season," he was saying to Starr, and then he was shaking hands with Zeke Bratkowski and, walking again, acknowledging the others. "Forrest...Boyd... Lionel...Jerry...Herb."

He walked into the trainer's room. Willie Wood and Tom Brown, the safety men, were sitting on one of the tables, waiting to be taped, and he walked up to Wood, four times an All-Pro.

"Willie," he said, "you can't play football with sideburns."

"You can't?" Wood said.

"Look around the league," he said, "and anyone with sideburns isn't worth a thing. Better get 'em off."

He walked back through the dressing room. As he was nearing the door he noticed Travis Williams, the halfback and kickoff return specialist, with a cigarette.

"You better watch those," he said. "How many a day?"

"A pack and a half," Williams said.

"That's terrible," he said.

He walked down the tunnel and stopped to check where paint was peeling on the edge of a crack. In the bright sunlight he walked across a corner of the field to tell the leader of the Packer band that, in subsequent games, the band would be stationed at the other end, and then he noticed the Packer kickers coming out onto the field to warm up.

"I'd better get out of here," he said, and, with those in the crowd near him calling to him now, he climbed the sixty rows to the top of the stands. In the press box, on the second deck, they have built a glass-fronted, air-conditioned, sound-proofed booth for him, with phone and TV monitor.

"This is all right," he was saying, sitting there and watching the teams warm up. "Real good, but look at that 76 of theirs. Bob Brown. Big and a good blocker, too. Willie Davis won't get to the passer today. This is all right here."

For 29 years, in high school, in the colleges and with the pros, he had known only the sideline. "In these last few years," his wife had said, "I couldn't look at him on the sideline. When he'd get mad and lose his temper I was afraid he'd have a heart attack, and I didn't tell him this until he quit, but I was afraid that some day he might be shot.

"There are a lot of nuts," she said, "and Vin bred violence. You win as much as we did, and people get mad at you."

He sat there now in silence. He watched Jerry Kramer kick off to the Eagle five and Alvin Haymond run it back to the 23.

"They'll run this first one right up the center," he said. "We've been giving up yardage there."

Izzy Lang took the handoff and made four yards up the middle. On the second play, Lang gained seven yards running to the strong side.

"The trap on Willie Davis," he said. "That big Bob Brown really seals off that whole side."

When the Packers held he said nothing. On their first offensive series, when Starr was hit and lost 17 yards and then, on the next play, threw a pass down the middle that Joe Scarpati intercepted and brought back to the Packer 37, he just took a deep breath and let it out.

"Here's a toss," he said, as Izzy Lang took it and made 10 yards off the right side. "Oh, dear. That Brown really clears the way. Come on, please."

Once more the Packers held. On fourth down, however, Sam Baker kicked a field goal from the 27, and it was Eagles 3, Packers 0.

"There's no zip," he said. "I mean it's flat. Maybe it's because I'm inside. You don't get the feeling here."

Herb Adderly took the kickoff on the goal line and ran it back to midfield.

"We can hurt you too many ways," he said. "Now here's a pass, the 84 Hook, probably. No."

It was the power sweep that he put in when he was offensive coach with the New York Giants and, more than any other, it is his play. Now they call it the Green Bay Sweep, and now, with Anderson carrying, it was going for nine yards.

"No one knows," he said once, "how much sweat, tears, driving and pushing goes into making that sweep go well. It's not a great play, but I could sell it to the players and they believed in it — and that's what made it a great play."

Now the Packers were moving. Jim Grabowski was running the slant that Jimmy Taylor ran so well and Starr was passing to Boyd Dowler and Marv Fleming and then Grabowski was in the end zone and Vince Lombardi was just sitting there, saying nothing.

"Congratulations, general manager," one of them waiting outside of his booth was saying to him after the Packers had won, 30-13. "How do you like it up here?"

"I don't," he said.

On the way down though the stands he signed some autographs, and when he got to the coaches' room there were eight reporters around Phil Bengtson and he skirted them. He went back into the players' dressing room and found Bart Starr and congratulated him and then he saw Willie Davis.

"He's a pretty good football player," he said, "that Brown."

"I'll tell you," Davis said. "On runs he just kinda chills you."

He went out to the office and Merrill Knowlton, the ticket director, told him that 30 people had reported losing their tickets and Tom Miller showed him the turnstile count. Then he got in his car and drove home.

In the old days, as old as a year ago, his mind would have been working over the ball game. He would have been changing the blocking on the 49 Toss or deciding to work them harder on the two-minute drill.

"Today," he was saying at home later, "I was wondering how I'm going to stay as far removed as I am. I felt I was in another world up there. You're just too far removed from the game.

"It's murder," he said. "I never knew I'd miss it as much."

23

The Epistle of St. Vincent
by Tom Dowling

"Vince Lombardi Vs. Will Loman" was the *Variety* headline on a story explaining how the sales industry is filming pep-talks by Lombardi to counteract its "Death of a Salesman" image. Arthur Miller might laugh, but the salesmen sit tall in their seats, each one a potential Bart Starr in a third-and-goal-to-go situation, with the coach up there on the screen flashing the go-ahead sign.

Lombardi is an Old Testament believer in sin and virtue, the unforgivability of failure and the exaltation of success. It is a harsh code, one which recognizes no middle ground.

Accordingly, Lombardi himself has been pictured largely in sinister blacks and new improved whiter than whites, as a sadist or a molder of men, as a fanatic or a superman.

Among those with the rosier view of Lombardi is the management of the Washington Redskins, a football team that in recent years has made Willy Loman look like a spectacular success. The Redskins hired Lombardi in February to turn an affable collection of underachievers into a winning football team, a sales force that would put the company over the top in such hitherto barren territory as New York, Dallas, Philadelphia, New Orleans, Cleveland and Atlanta. The Redskins did what any failing organization must do to break out of the cycle of despair — they hired themselves a legend. As head coach, general manager and part-owner, they have

Vince Lombardi, builder of world champions, probably the finest coach in football, and certainly the most dominating personality in sports.

Until the new season begins, Lombardi is only as good as his record. So I flew to Green Bay, Wis., to find out what the Redskins had bought, to see how much of the Lombardi legend is black and how much is white, and to study the code Lombardi had set for himself and find out whether he had lived up to it.

Spring comes late to northern Wisconsin. As the plane closed on Green Bay, I could see the trees budding and fresh green in the farmland below. The man next to me, a businessman from a small town north of Green Bay, was assuring me that "the Pack would be back," that the team's dismal 6-7-1 record in 1968 without Coach Lombardi in command was just one of those things.

As for the Redskins, Lombardi would shape them up in a hurry. Had I read about the off-field carousing of Redskin quarterback Sonny Jurgensen in *The Saturday Evening Post* a year ago? I had. Had I noticed Sonny's jellybelly on the TV games? I had. Well, he ventured, Sonny would be well advised to do something about that gut. Diet. Go on the wagon. That spare-tire was not something Coach Lombardi would warm up to.

Jurgensen's stomach was to prove a continuing *leitmotif* during my Green Bay stay. Some Packer fans regarded it as a direct personal affront to Coach Lombardi; others as a minor indiscretion that would have to be dealt with understandingly, yet firmly. From the viewpoint of the Green Bay citizenry, themselves built on almost Bavarian proportions, Jurgensen's stomach was apparently the most familiar landmark in the Nation's Capital. It was a protuberance symbolizing the slack luxury of the effete East Coast. No wonder the nation was in deep trouble, the younger generation going to the dogs. What could you expect when the quarterback, the field general, the leader of the football team in the very capital of the nation had run to seed, like a pudgy general in some Latin American junta?

It was in this xenophobic atmosphere that Lombardi's winning brand of football was nurtured. And yet there was the irony that Lombardi himself was an Easterner, a city boy from Brooklyn. This fact nagged at many. Green Bay wanted a winner, but they were loath to have an outsider, an Easterner, produce it for them. So they pretended Lombardi was a homegrown boy, deliriously happy down on the farm.

Sometimes, though, the truth stared them in the face. A friend of Lombardi's told me that once he had been in Coach's room in The Drake Hotel in Chicago before a Bears' game. Lombardi was standing at the window, looking down at the Outer Drive and the lights reflected on Lake Michigan. "C'mere," Lombardi grunted. The man walked over to the window. "Look at that," Lombardi commanded. "What about it?" the man said. "You don't have anything like that in Green Bay," Lombardi said. "You're damn right we don't," the man said. "What do you mean?" Lombardi asked, startled at the counterattack. "Vince," the man said, "you've never had it so good, never been as happy anywhere as you've been in Green Bay." Lombardi hung his head, but the truth was out. Coach had a hankering for the outside world. Green Bay, Fox River was all right, but it wasn't the Outer Drive, with the lights of the skyscrapers glittering in Lake Michigan.

My seatmate chortled to himself as he continued to ponder Sonny Jurgensen's stomach. Lombardi will take care of Jurgensen, he concluded. Coach always gets 110 percent from his players. He seems to believe the figure means something. He has convinced millions of Americans that his ominous, growling requests for 110 percent have been met in full, that his players perform miracles, that enemy lines part like the Red Sea when his players smell the goal line. The credibility gap has never been a problem for Vince Lombardi. "Football is a game of cliches," he has written, "and I believe in every one of them."

Lombardi took over the ailing Green Bay Packers in 1959. He was forty-five years old and was known, if only to bubblegum card collectors, as one of the "Seven Blocks of Granite" in the Fordham line during the middle 1930s. He played right guard at 172 pounds. He was not an all-American.

After leaving Fordham Law School one year short after graduation, Lombardi labored from 1938 to 1946 in the vineyards of high school coaching at St. Cecilia in Englewood, New Jersey. At one point, his teams won thirty-six straight games. From 1946 to 1948, he was an assistant coach at Fordham, and for six more years an assistant at West Point under Colonel Earl "Red" Blaik, of whom Lombardi has written: "Whatever success I have must be attributed to the 'Old Man.' He molded my methods and my whole approach to the game. . . if there is a No. 1 coach of all time, in my opinion, it is Colonel Blaik."

"Lombardi is a thoroughbred with a vile temper," Blaik observed of his protege. Assistant coaches under Blaik had a way of moving up as head coaches elsewhere — Stu Holcomb to Purdue, Andy Gustafson to Miami, Bob Woodruff to Florida, Bobby Dodd to Tulsa, Murray Warmath to Minnesota. It didn't work out that way for Lombardi, who left West Point in 1954 to become an assistant coach once again — this time with the New York Giants.

"I wanted to be a head coach at a large university," Lombardi wrote two years ago. "The offers I had were from schools that were too small or from larger ones that were de-emphasizing football. I know I lost some jobs because of my Italian heritage."

And so it happened, whether through discrimination, or vile temper, or bad luck, that Vince Lombardi was forty-five when he became a head coach for the first time. (Knute Rockne was thirty when he took over Notre Dame.)

The Green Bay Packers were 4-8 in 1956, 3-9 in 1957, 1-10-1 in 1958. In 1959, their first year under Lombardi, the Packers finished 7-5. In the first game of that season they beat their traditional rivals, the Chicago Bears, 9-6, and Packer players carried Lombardi off the field on their shoulders.

In the next eight years, Lombardi's Packers won six Western Division titles, five N.F.L. championships (three in a row from 1965-67), and two Super Bowls. While Lombardi was head coach, the Packers scored 3,080 points in season play; their opponents 1,874. That works out to a Packer average of 25.3 a game; 14.5 for the opposition. The Packer's were eight-tenths of a point better than the classic ten-point spread a coach must play for as the margin of protection. There is something almost Newtonian in the clockwork sense of cosmic order and purpose contained in that eight-tenths of a point. Small wonder Las Vegas bookies used to say Lombardi meant "points" when the odds on a game were figured.

Among football fans, there is some division of opinion over the

finest football team of all time; some believe it was the 1962
Packers, others the Packer squad of 1966. Both were destroyers,
remorseless in the fourth quarter. Though the players were largely
the same, the teams were vastly different. The 1962 Packers were
young and over-powering; the 1966 version experienced, cunning
and resourceful. They were both trained, like jungle cats, to possess
what Lombardi has called "this ravenous appetite for success."
They were teams that had the mark of the lion's paw, the Lombardi
touch.

In Green Bay, I found that the myths, platitudes and misinforma-
tion about Lombardi had already been codified into a sort of canon
law. And why not? He was already referred to as St. Vincent.

"Coach Lombardi is a legend in his own time," a member of the
Packer official family told me, pausing to make certain I recorded
this insight for posterity. "He had success written all over him.
. . . He never let us down on anything."

"How about the earthy side of the man?" I asked.

"I never heard the man swear in my life," he said. I was to hear
some strange things in Green Bay. But nothing stranger, more
preposterous than this — not even from the Packer linen concession
man who said the team used thirteen thousand towels during a muddy
game with Cleveland.

No, if there is one thing certain about Lombardi it is that he a
prodigious swearer, a "ranter and raver" as his players call him, an
indefatigable and stentorian curser of men. Last year, for example,
during the threatened players' strike, Lee Remmel, who covers the
Packers for the *Green Bay Press Gazette,* dropped by the veterans'
voluntary workout at a local high school field. He was suddenly
stopped in his tracks by a trumpet volley of curses. Even Remmel,
used to ferocious Lombardi outbursts, was taken aback. But the
odd thing was that while the words were pure Lombardi, the voice
was not. Lee Roy Caffey, the Packer's veteran linebacker, came
trotting over. "Coach isn't here today, Lee," he explained. "I just
thought I'd make you feel at home."

The man who never heard Lombardi swear was not alone in re-
shaping the legend. The real facts were rapidly sinking into the rich
loam of small-town myth. Lombardi had ruled Green Bay with an
iron hand for ten years, and not that he was gone his detractors and

apologists were hard at work altering the legend to their own needs. Yet, I was to find out, even the detractors had to fall back on magnification in order to reduce Lombardi to size. There was only one way to belittle the man and that was to raise him up to a plane of absurdity. To demean Lombardi was to tarnish the beloved Packers, to diminish doughty Green Bay, the all-American city of 75,000 plain-living citizens who had financed and fielded the greatest football team of all time.

The Packers were the religion of Green Bay, and Lombardi, though gone to the Great Beyond of Washington, was still its saint.

"You should have seen the canonization when he left," I was told. "There must have been five thousand people at the testimonial dinner for St. Vincent. Max McGee (rake, prankster, twelve-year veteran end, and a Lombardi favorite) walked out on stage with loaves and fish on a platter. Vince laughed like hell. Well, why wouldn't he? The truth never hurts."

The Lombardi home in Green Bay was sold to a local psychiatrist. "Vince asked $56,000 and got $56,000," said a man who knew the new owner. I expressed surprise at the purchaser's cowed bargaining. The man shrugged. "You don't dicker with God," he deadpanned.

My informant's wife broke into the conversation. "After the Lombardis moved out, the psychiatrist's wife had all her girl friends come around and go over the place with a fine-toothed comb, from top to bottom."

What were they looking for?" I asked.

"Relics," she said with delight. "Holy relics."

Henry Jordan, the Packers' five-time All-Pro defensive tackle, sat behind the bare desk of his Green Bay mortgage company examining the progress of his portfolio in *The Wall Street Journal.* I had brought along a Packer publicity still for him to autograph for my son. The photo made Jordan look like an enraged, bald-headed bear clawing a tourist's car in Yellowstone after having been fed a tin can. In his office Jordan was a gentle man, witty, almost courtly. "You know," Jordan said, peering into the palm of his hand, "I'll tell you something about Coach. (Lombardi is called Coach. Not the coach, or Coach Lombardi, but Coach.) A couple of years back I had this terrible rash on my hand, getting worse and worse. The

Packers sent me to five specialists and they couldn't do a thing. I could see the bone, it got so bad. Even with bandaging I'd be doing pushups at practice and a blade of grass would touch that wound and I'd holler like a baby. One day Coach comes up to me. 'Here,' he says real gruff and hands me this little unmarked bottle of liquid. 'Use this.' So I figured, what the hell. Two days later, the rash started to heal." Jordan thrust out the giant hand for me to see, a miracle prop in an Oral Roberts tent-meeting.

"I'll tell you another thing," Jordan went on. "One day it's raining at training camp. I'm sort of walking by Coach, minding my own business. Suddenly he looks up at the sky and says, 'Stop raining, Goddamn it.' There's a flash of lightning, some thunder and then it stops. He looks at me and I look at him. Well, I've been eating fish on Fridays ever since, and I'm a Methodist."

A favorite Packer story about Lombardi is the night he went home after a long practice session in the cold, climbed into bed with his wife, Marie, and she said "God, your feet are cold."

"Dear," he said, "in the privacy of the house you may call me Vince."

The greater the saint, the sweeter the incense, the proverb goes. But the incense is, after all, burned in offering to the legend, to the saint's ultimate meaning to the faithful, and not to the complexities and contradictions of his daily existence.

And so it was that Lombardi injunctions from the Book of St. Vincent were meant to polarize in their absolutism, bound to produce jeers or adulation. A few sample Lombardi admonitions:

"There are three important things in life: Family, Religion and the Green Bay Packers."

"Fatigue makes cowards of us all."

"You've got to be mentally tough."

"There is no substitute for work."

"Everything is want in this business. The man who wants to play is the man I want."

"There is only one yardstick in our business and that is winning. Second place is meaningless."

"I will try to make of each of you the best football player he can possibly be. I will try with every fiber in me, and I will try and try and try."

Before going to Green Bay I had read all of the available book and magazine Lombardiana. As a fan I had watched the televised drama of the Packer's great championship games over the years — a drama, we were all reminded by zoom shots, that was staged by the sheer will power of the squat Italian-American standing on the sideline in the fur cap and camel hair overcoat. It seemed that, on the record at least, Lombardi's central qualities were a monolithic ego and formidable intelligence, a spiritual hunger that bordered on religiosity, and a natural exuberance that he distrusted and refused to value except as an instrument to lead men.

The ego had forged his indomitable pride, his extraordinary sensitivity about himself (matched by an equally extraordinary insensitivity to others), his ambition, his decisiveness and his combative need to win. His intelligence had taught him self-control and had allowed him to fashion the fundamentals of football into a compact and highly organized system. His spiritual side was grounded in order and unyielding faith; it was not for nothing that Fordham taught its sons the texts of St. Thomas Aquinas and St. Augustine. He demanded loyalty and the acceptance of order. His spiritual faith led him to reduce moral issues to black and white, to give him a strong didactic streak, and to infuse him with an absolute disregard for pain and discomfort. His exuberance allowed him to communicate with his team, to bend them to his will, to make him in the end, for all his dictatorial qualities and pettiness, a "likeable bastard."

These are traits of both considerable virtue and potential danger. Circumstances can make them go either way. For they are traits that can break men. He is a man then who truly seems to hinge on success or failure. If his teams are winners they owe it all to Lombardi — their money, their fame and their pride. If his teams are losers, that is Lombardi's doing as well and there will be jackals laying in wait. Forty football players will pay the Lombardi price of anguish, humiliation, and bodily punishment to win, but not to lose.

The Packers are the oldest franchise in the N.F.L., founded in 1919 by Curly Lambeau with jerseys provided by the Indian Packing Company. Lambeau was to remain as head coach for thirty years. Some of his Packer teams were great ones and six were N.F.L. champions.

When Curly Lambeau died in 1967, there was considerable local sentiment for renaming the city stadium after him. The team's nominal rulers, the seven-man executive committee, thought it a fitting tribute, but Lombardi demurred. Call it Green Bay Stadium, he suggested. No one knew who Curly Lambeau was anymore. Why have TV announcers mumbling Curly Lambeau Field, when they could just as easily give Green Bay a little national exposure. Lombardi was overruled by the executive committee, some said for the first time, and Lambeau Field it is. Cynics might say, and did, that it grated Lombardi to play on a field named after his predecessor.

I took a cab out to Lambeau Field, located at 1265 Lombardi Avenue, to talk to the players and coaches who had worked for Lombardi. Lombardi memorabilia were pointed out to me: the League's first wall-to-wall carpeted dressing room, the divot in the conference room carpet where Coach had erected a golf net to perfect his game ("You know," he once said, "with my temperament I could have been a great professional golfer, except for one thing — I can't play golf very well."), the three-tiered sauna bath with benches like Roman banquet couches. Outside the sauna there is a little legend Lombardi had posted above a tin box. "This sauna control is automatic and should not be touched."

"Of course, it wasn't automatic at all," publicity director Chuck Lane told me. "The players used to change the thermostat to their desired heat. So Coach had the thermostat returned to *his* favorite temperature and built this little tin box over the thing so it would stay just the way he liked it three hundred and sixty-five days a year." Lane took me for a tour of the stadium. The Packer management was talking about building an all-weather dome complete with Astroturf. They had to come up with some money-squandering scheme to spend what I was authoritatively told was $3.2 million in liquid assets.

One such "improvement" was the new press box high above the stadium. The windows on all but one of the boxes were louvered. "The window that's sealed up is where Coach used to sit last year when he was general manager," Lane explained. "Why is that," I joked, "so Lombardi wouldn't jack open the window and yell down: 'Bengtson, you dumb son-of-a-bitch, you shouldn't have used a 4-3 defense on that play?' " Lane gave me one of those looks that said you're not as dumb as you look.

It was on Lambeau Field that Lombardi had put his Biblical precept to work, where he had driven his players through the endless repetition of grass drills, wind-sprints, calisthenics, and the finely-honed routine of blocking and tackling that was his style of football.

"There's shape and there's Lombardi shape," Henry Jordan told me. "Lombardi shape's when there's no sweat on your jersey in the fourth quarter when you've been in all afternoon. Shape's the guy across the line from you — the sweat dripping and the eyes glassy."

"Coach drives players hard, himself harder," said assistant coach Dave "Hawg" Hanner, a Packer tackle when Lombardi took over in 1959. Hanner should know. He had his appendix cut out some years back and Lombardi had him suited up on the football field twelve days later. Gale Gillingham, the Packer left offensive guard, broke his hand in the College All-Star camp and was released from the squad as injured. Drafted by the Packers, he reported to their training camp and started practicing the next day.

"I had a shoulder separation," Packer halfback Elijah Pitts said. "In college I wouldn't have dreamed of putting my uniform on. Here I didn't dare tell Coach I had it. I was afraid to tell him. I played two games with it." Lionel Aldridge, the Packer end, broke his leg. He was supposed to wear a cast for six weeks. Two weeks later he was working out.

"Hurt is in the mind," Lombardi says, quoting his father Harry.

This is the Lombardi legend, the tyrant with the rictus-grin torturing his post-collegian innocents, rallying the crippled, and dying for one last goal line stand. There is some truth in this, and there is truth, as well, in the essential masochism of the players. Many of them enjoy pain as a way of pushing their masculinity beyond human limits.

I was told that when Paul Hornung and Max McGee were roommates they used to stage a ritual game of breaking Lombardi's curfew rules. One night they drew their single beds together, undressed, and when Lombardi made the 11 p.m. bed check, he found the pair of them grinning up at him, naked in one another's arms. "Jesus Christ," he is supposed to have said, "you guys *do* need a night on the town." Freudians may gasp, but the point is that football players live in a realm that is beyond guilt, doubts and pain. "You've got to be mentally tough," Lombardi says, and when a football player loses that supreme confidence in his super-masculinity, he is in deep trouble.

"When Vin gets one he thinks can be a real good ballplayer," Marie Lombardi said, "I feel sorry for that boy. Vince will just open a hole in that boy's head and pour everything he knows into it, and there's no way out of it. I don't want to watch it."

What Mrs. Lombardi does not want to watch is Vince the psychologist at work. His psychological mastery of others suggests a quality of guile, of deliberation, of mandarin patience. It is a quality far removed from the stereotyped picture of Lombardi, the fiery, impetuous castigator striking out at players at random. At bottom, Lombardi is more plodding, more supple and Byzantine than he appears on the surface.

One of the staples of the Lombardi legend is the trade that sent the Packers' seven-time All-Pro center Jim Ringo to the Philadelphia Eagles. Ringo arrived to talk contract with Lombardi accompanied by a lawyer. This is my lawyer, Ringo said, I brought him since I don't know much about business matters. Excuse me for a moment, Lombardi said, leaving the room. Five minutes later he came back and addressed the lawyer. I am afraid, Lombardi said, you have come to the wrong city to discuss Mr. James Ringo's contract. Mr. James Ringo is now the property of the Philadelphia Eagles.

A good story, but it puzzled me. First of all, Ringo was a Lombardi style player — hard-nosed, 110 percent, all desire, underweight for a pro lineman. He was also an aging All-Pro, but still had good market value. He was said to be moody, something of a clubhouse lawyer, the sort of man who might let it be known that he was planning to stick it to Coach when contract time came around. Lombardi, who maintained a sort of oriental espionage network in the dressing room, was probably a step ahead of Ringo. Would it not be the apotheosis of craft to trade Ringo while he was still good value, to thereby psychologically petrify any other contract bandits at the same time, and to cap the whole affair with an aphoristic exchange with Ringo's lawyer that would make good press copy for years to come? The Packers got twenty-three-year-old linebacker Lee Roy Caffey for Ringo. Ringo has been retired for several years;

Caffey, an All-Pro, has six or seven years of football left in him.

I asked Lombardi about the Ringo trade, if it had happened in the five-minute time span that legend proclaimed. He gave me a Fu Man Chu scowl. "Hell no. That's no way to general manage a football team." Might not the Jim Ringo trade have been signed and sealed before Ringo and his lawyer tapped on the general manager's door, I inquired? He gave me a grin. "Yeah, something like that," he said.

Henry Jordan provided still another insight into Lombardi's endless patience and plotting. One day Jordan was passing by Coach's office before a practice session and, peering in, saw Lombardi at his desk making hideous grimaces. "I poked my head in, trying to figure who he was looking at. Damned if he wasn't all alone, trying to get himself mad at us, I guess. That sort of thing takes a lot out of Coach."

It occurred to me that Lombardi resorted to such legerdemain because he was certain that Somebody up there liked him, because he knew Somebody would understand that the black magic he worked on his fellowman served some worthy goal. Lombardi is a devout Catholic. He attends mass every day, and even takes priests along on road trips. Though he claims it is the team's idea, the Packers pray together in the dressing room before and after a game. "We don't pray to win," Lombardi has written, "I do think we pray to play the best we can and to keep us free from injury. And the prayer we say after the game is one of Thanksgiving." There are also devotional meetings on Sunday morning. Carrol Dale, Willie Davis and Bart Starr read from the Bible and lead the prayers; occasionally a visiting spiritual luminary gives a speech. A player told me attendance has been falling off lately, but that last year Lombardi was booked to address the group and all the players who had been with the club since 1959 showed up.

Perhaps it was that battle-tested faith, that absence of niggling doubts that made the Lombardi Packers a happy team. And they were happy, there is no doubt of that. There was all that Super Bowl loot, the endorsements, the banquet circuit fees, the outside business deals, the swag and swagger of championships. But it went deeper than that. "You knew where you stood with Coach," a player told me. "He took care of everything for you — so there was no worrying, no bickering, no cheap shit, just football to concentrate on."

The Packers are about 40 percent black and 60 percent white, and they are an integrated society at ease with one another. Rookies are assigned roommates in alphabetical order; Lombardi saw to that. Marv Fleming, a black tight end, arrived at training camp in 1967 and with a big grin flashed calling cards that said Muhammad Fleming. That was the summer of Newark and Detroit. Later that summer the Packers were playing an exhibition in Cleveland, where racial tensions were flaring. Down in the dressing room someone had pasted bumper stickers proclaiming "Polish Power" over the locker of Zeke Bratkowski, white, and Elijah Pitts, black. The Poles were a dirty word in Cleveland's black ghetto that week, the blacks a dirtier one in the city's East European blue-collar neighborhoods. The Packers roared with laughter. And why not? Hadn't the team once given Lombardi a T-shirt to take on a hunting trip with a bull's-eye on the back bearing the words "Italian target." And hadn't Coach laughed like hell in that hunting lodge in Upper Michigan when he opened the surprise package?

Packer coach Phil Bengston sits behind a spheroid-shaped desk in the stadium-long office he has inherited, furnishings and all, from Lombardi.

"In 1959, Vince's first year," Bengtson told me, "we played an exhibition game down South. The white players and the black players were booked into different hotels, couldn't eat in the same restaurant. That's the last time that ever happened. Vince let the traveling secretary know that if a town wanted the Green Bay Packers, they got all of them in the same hotel and at the same training table. And that's the way it's always been."

With his players, Lombardi had no obligation to observe the small civilities of life. There was no room for equality between player and coach, underling and boss. So I talked with members of the Packer seven-man executive committee (the team is a community-owned, non-profit corporation with 4,738½ shares held by 1,698 shareholders who receive no dividends), Lombardi's friends, and Green Bay sportswriters. These were men, I thought, for whom he had no need to practice those solitary grimaces, men who might have seen him waver from the single-minded code of self-discipline and success, men who might have had occasion to notice a crack in the facade.

Lombardi's intimate circle of friends were known as the "trained seals." I found them approachable, generous, articulate, radiating self-confidence and success, and invariably obsessed with the Great Man. Now that he had departed, they were reorganizing the void in their lives and they had something of the dolorous quality of drunken Irishmen.

Stories abounded of their washing his golf balls on the links, of Coach yawning at a TV program and his friends bounding to their feet in unison to switch channels and denounce the fatuousness of the fare they had been chuckling at moments earlier. "When Vince laughed, the seals roared," a member of the entourage told me.

And yet, there were special dispensations where Lombardi and his friends were concerned. His friends were small-town men and proud of it, and while they were rich and successful, they were still a little astonished to be buddies with one of the greatest men in America.

Lombardi was a windfall none of them could have predicted for themselves and so they counted their blessings and brought out the worst side of his monumental ego. They laughed at his jokes, applauded his gall and called it charm, washed his golf balls and called it friendship.

I wondered if Lombardi's special affection for Paul Hornung and Max McGee didn't have something to do with the fact that both were lip-offs in a gentle boyish sort of way. Then, too, by their very wildness Hornung and McGee brought out Lombardi's reformist zeal, the old Italian *pater familias* pride in the prodigal sons who drank raw red wine through the long hours of the night down at the village cantina and rose promptly at dawn to attend mass before trudging off to the fields for ten hour's backbreaking work. Lombardi loved their irreverence toward him. Perhaps he felt that boys should have spunk, and that grown men should be serious, even worshipful.

His grown friends were all of that and tenaciously loyal as well. There are not many men who command loyalty to the degree Lombardi does and for that matter, not many who preach it with his Savonarola-like intensity. Loyalty is the very heart of the Lombardi code. He demands it of his players and takes pride in returning it. At bottom, it was team loyalty that had made the Packers the invincible beast of the National Football League. He loved football, Lombardi told me, because it taught men loyalty to an entity greater than themselves.

Before I went to Green Bay I had heard that Lombardi's abrupt departure to Washington was regarded as a betrayal or at least a deviation from the rigid code of loyalty. I had heard that Lombardi's friends were heartbroken at the furtive manner of his departure, the back-room arrangements worked out with Edward Bennett Williams, the Redskin president, and Pete Rozelle, the N.F.L. commissioner.

"Of course, he was happy here," one friend went on, "but every one of us wants a little something he can call his own. So, when the chance came to get a piece of the action in Washington, Vince had to go. What the hell, you want to have something to leave the kids when you die. You can't call that disloyalty. He had to go. He was happy here, never been happier in his life." The man's voice was torn with emotion.

"To Oley — for his contribution to the Packers and his sympathy and loyalty to me, Vince." So reads the inscription on the smiling ink portrait of Lombardi on the office wall of Packer president Dominic Olejniczak.

"How about the loyalty issue," I asked Olejniczak, a real estate entrepreneur and former Green Bay mayor. "Wasn't it true," I said, "that in 1961, when Wellington Mara of the New York Giants wanted Lombardi for head coach, he contacted you as president of the Packers to get permission to sound out Lombardi for the job?"

"That's right," Olejniczak said, "that was the way it happened in 1961. Vince wanted to take the Giant job, the executive committee turned him down, and he stayed on and continued to do a great job for us."

"Well, then," I said, "when Lombardi asked to be released from his Green Bay contract to go with the Redskins there was no consultation with the executive committee, as there had been in the Mara feeler in 1961. Lombardi had pretty clearly hammered the arrangement out in advance with Edward Bennett Williams and Pete Rozelle before seeking his release."

"Vince was not disloyal. He was general manager of the club, and as such could be approached legitimately by Williams."

"He was also general manager when Mara asked for him," I reminded him.

Olejniczak glared at me and then with a thin smile said, "Let's just say that Wellington Mara is one kind of man and Edward Bennett Williams is another."

I raised the loyalty issue with Dick Bourguignon, a Lombardi intimate and vice president of the Packers. Bourguignon is a big, shambling man. He struck me as the most reflective of Lombardi's close friends. "I think Vince stepped down as head coach after the '67 season because he was drained, worried about his health — perhaps too much had come his way too fast — and, of course, he stayed on as general manager and perhaps he should have known and his friends should have known that he'd never be happy out of coaching. Anyway, the executive committee's agreement with Vince was that he couldn't coach another team, but we said we wouldn't stand in his way if he could get part interest in another club — somehow it never occurred to us he might combine the coaching and ownership. . . ."

"He sort of found a loophole, a kind of moral tax shelter?" I asked, thinking that Lombardi's two years in Fordham Law School had not been wasted, after all. Or maybe it was Edward Bennett Williams, who had brushed up on his corporate law to scrutinize the terms of Lombardi's gentleman's agreement with Green Bay.

Bourguignon smiled non-committally.

"Do you suppose," I asked Bourguignon, "that the injection of the loyalty issue made Lombardi's decision to leave Green Bay the only non-black and white moral issue he ever faced? The first time he saw gray?"

"No," he said, "Vince never had time to see gray, he made up his mind too fast for that."

"Why did Lombardi go to the Redskins?" I asked Bengtson. "A chance to own part of a ballclub, a need to get back into coaching combined with the knowledge that to do it here would mean you would have to go, a sort of spiritual need to redeem another failure of a team, a sense that the Nation's Capital was a place that could use a winner at long last?"

"Yeah, those are some pretty good reasons," he said. For a fraction of a second he shook his head, as if to say, "They're damn good reasons all right, but for Lombardi they just aren't adequate!"

Bishop Aloysius Wycislo is the prelate of Green Bay, which is seventy-five percent Catholic. I was late for my appointment. It was the Bishop's day off and he was taking the air in the backyard of the immense caboose-red brick residence. It was one of those heavy Victorian piles, thrown up across the Midwest in the late nineteenth century. Inside, the institutional carpeting, Morris chairs, antimacassars, Victorian chests, and wardrobes as large as sea-ships proclaimed a Catholic world where the Pope was still infallible, pill and all.

I was ushered into the Bishop's study and when he joined me I made an apologetic joke about not adhering to "Lombardi time." ("There is time and Lombardi time," according to Jerry Kramer.)

The Bishop, in a blue short-sleeved shirt, had a high-buffed color in his face and gray wavy hair, the kind Paul Hornung might have in ten years time. "I didn't know Vince all that well," he began, "though I've seen him socially and we've worked together on charitable causes for the church. I suppose you read what I said at the airport when I arrived?"

I admitted I hadn't.

"There was a crowd of welcomers there, and as the TV cameras started to grind, Vince stepped up with a sealed envelope. Inside was a Packer season pass. So I said, 'Apparently, judging from the enthusiasm shown over this season pass you bring to me, you must consider it more important than the Papal Bull that the Holy Father in Rome gave me to bring here to you."

It occurred to me they may have had a good laugh over that sally back at the Vatican, but in Green Bay, with twenty thousand fans on the waiting list for season tickets, you could swap three Papal Bulls and two Apostolic Briefs for one ticket in the end zone.

Having established the primacy of the Church over the Packers in his own mind, the Bishop relaxed. He had obviously done a lot of thinking about Lombardi, and was fond of him. "Vince was an old-fashioned Catholic," he told me. "When he'd see me, he'd ask to kiss my ring. I'd joke and say, 'You don't have to do that. It'll only get you ninety days indulgence and football season won't even have begun by then.' 'No,' Vince would say, 'I still want to do it.' "

I noted that Lombardi had once been a seminarian, studying for the priesthood. Would he have made a good priest?

"Yes," the Bishop said. "There is an underlying compassion in the man. This is going to sound peculiar in light of his ego and his temper, but there is a manly humility about him as well. He is a man of tremendous will. He is able to control his life, yet able to let go, to reveal himself — perhaps deliberately — so that people sense some extra quality about him. Before he left I was going to ask him to talk to the priests going through an identity crisis. They respected him."

"Was Lombardi a happy man?" I asked.

The Bishop swiveled in his chair and regarded the wall. "No," he finally said, "I don't think so." He turned back to stare at me. "I think in the whole time I knew him I only saw him happy, truly at ease, just once. It was at a party after a football game and I can't even recall whether the Packers won or lost, but some friends from his Fordham days were in town. They were playing a word game in Latin, in which the declined endings were cleverly disguised to score points at one another's expense. Your Latin had to be first-rate to play the game and Vince was reveling at it. His Latin was excellent."

I pressed ahead on the loyalty front. No, the Bishop didn't think Lombardi had acted with disloyalty. There were, he said, people in Green Bay who judged Lombardi harshly, who harped on the loyalty theme, who were suspicious of Lombardi as an Easterner.

Finally the Bishop said: "You know, a boy serving mass told me, 'I guess he should go, but how can he be disloyal? It's a good thing for him, my parents say, but I can't believe he'd do it.' "

The Bishop and I mulled that one over. It had a certain finality. Out of the past came the voice of the small boy staring up at Shoeless Joe Jackson after the Black Sox scandal and saying: "Say it ain't so, Joe."

The Bishop seemed unruffled. After all, the Church existed because men were flawed.

It occurred to me that if Lombardi had wanted to get off that loyalty petard he had hoisted himself upon in Green Bay there was a graceful way: politics. Yes, the call to higher duty. He could have "heeded the call" to public office. Lombardi was clearly a man with a volcano inside him, a sense of destiny, a capacity to move and deeply influence men, a man even Lyndon Johnson would have been happy to go to the well with. He had endorsed Senator Gaylord Nelson's re-election bid and he is now an active proponent of President Nixon's Safeguard A.B.M. system. On Vietnam, a close friend of Lombardi's told me that Coach had been critical of the war long before Vietnam became unpopular. When I asked Lombardi about this, he said he had never been against anything "American." He had been offered the lieutenant governor's nomination on the Wisconsin Democratic ticket in 1968, and some said he was even building a state power base for the governorship by entering the public housing development field. It must have tempted Lombardi, a man interested in the exercise of power, the intellect and the spirit, a man who in his way was the Cardinal Richelieu of the gridiron.

My own hunch is that Lombardi, like most of us, is uncomfortable in a milieu that is strange to him and that he cannot knowledgeably dominate from the outset. Perhaps this is why he went into coaching in the first place, rather than finishing the law degree that would have been an uncommon asset in the mid-1930's for a poor Italian boy from Brooklyn.

Then, too, there was that image of Lombardi high in The Drake Hotel scanning the Chicago lakefront. "I was at a party with Vince once," a friend told me. "It had been going on for an hour or so, everybody having a good time. Then this sudden look came over Vince's face. 'I think I'll have that first drink now," he said. You can't imagine the intensity of that look, as if somehow he had been holding himself back, holding himself back all of his life." Was Washington — the capital of the world, as Lombardi has called it — what he had been holding off for?

After I returned from Green Bay, I went to the Redskin offices to interview Lombardi. My telephone conversations with Redskin officialdom arranging for the interview were punctuated with the familiar "Coach is..." and "Coach says..." and "Coach informs me..." Coach is always a reverential tone lower than the other words in the sentence. Sonny Jurgenson was making a phone call in the office next to Lombardi's. The papers said Sonny referred to Coach as "Mr. Lombardi" and that his social life was said to be fastidiously correct.

If I needed any reminder of the differences between the Midwest

and the East, the contrasts between the Redskin offices on Connect-
icut Avenue and the Packer headquarters on Lombardi Avenue provided it.

In Green Bay, the Packer staff had been open, obliging, cheerful.
Here, in Washington, even the secretaries gave me sour looks. The
executive offices are protected by black wrought-iron lattice-work
gates at either end of the hallway.

In Green Bay, the offices, aside from Lombardi's are Spartan and
cramped, with humble masonite on the floors. The Redskin offices
are egalitarian in their plush pomposity. They seem to step from the
pages of some curious *New Yorker* ad where all of the products
featured in the magazine have been photographed together in the
same room — the Bigelows on the floor, the Steuben cut glass
ashtrays on the Cambridge Design coffee tables.

If Lombardi's office in Green Bay resembled a Presidential Suite
in a Midwest motel, his Washington hideaway seemed the Hilton
Hotel's version. The Prussian blue fabrics and dark-stained
mahogany furniture created an atmosphere even more forbidding
than the Bishop's residence in Green Bay. Lombardi is a man of
character and it struck me as peculiar that he would choose to work
in offices devoid of it, each in their own way.

Lombardi is now fifty-six years old. During our first interview he
was working at his desk in shirtsleeves when I came in; there was a
blue VTL monogram over his breast. He had a modest pile of
papers on his desk which he continued to scratch away at throughout the interview. I had the impression they were not documents of
any moment and that by laboring over them he was fulfilling some
Puritan need to make wise use of his time.

His teeth and his eyes are his strongest features. From pictures, I
had expected him to be gap-toothed. But his teeth are set fairly close
together. They are just so large and dice-shaped that you tend to see
them as individual units, rather than as a set. Behind the glasses the
eyes are unusually volatile and expressive. His changes of mood are
dramatically sudden and you can read them instantly in the eyes.

My first session with Lombardi was brief, limited to questions
and answers, without much eye contact, with him scribbling away at
his papers and me trying to overcome the feeling of being a low-
draft choice meeting Coach for the first time. The second session

was much longer, without paperwork on his part; it was, in fact, a conversation. On that second visit, he was talking with his wife on the telephone squawk box when I came in. She talked for a while and then said: "Vince, I've got a very big favor to ask you. . ." The hand shot across the desk, banged off the squawk box, and he cradled the receiver to his ear. It was all done with startling, unconscious efficiency. I remembered hearing in Green Bay that Coach occasionally performed card tricks.

And I remembered Dick Bourguignon telling me, "Vince's timing is beautiful, always just beautiful." Whatever the favor Mrs. Lombardi had in mind, it was finally granted, though in rather glum tones.

During both sessions I asked about Lombardi's background, football, the generation gap, violence, Vietnam, Black Power, freedom and license, and loyalty. I was not so much interested in what he said as how he said it. I had already heard and read enough of what he had said, but filtered through the eyes of others.

He is not an easy man to talk to. He answered my questions directly, often at length, often with style, and always I felt with honesty. Yet there was a quality of reserve and suspicion, more than the guarded habits of a public man fearful of being misquoted in the press. For, as I said, his answers were forthcoming and some of what he said could have, if taken out of context, been used devastating against him. Perhaps his suspicion was directed inwardly, was prompted by his insecurity, the fear that the "facade would crack."

When he spoke of football, of Green Bay, and of his background, he was forceful and eloquent. Too much so, as if these were answers reeled off many times before. When he spoke about the young, the racial situation, the turmoil everywhere, he was surprisingly humane and reflective. There was none of the fire-eating halftime rhetoric, none of the sales pitches to revive the flagging spirits of the United States sales industry. Much of what he said was not well thought out, not aphoristic, but it expressed an attitude and a concern that no decent man need fear seeing in print with his name attached to it.

I asked why he had left the seminary. I half expected some bombast on how he had always regretted not being a priest. Instead he said, "You've got to have a vocation. That's why I wasn't a priest. As for why I went to Fordham, I was trying to get a football scholarship to college and they gave me one." I asked what he had learned in his years at West Point. "West Point taught me discipline, regularity, I guess you'd say order. Red Blaik taught me the meaning of organization." And then what? "And then Green Bay taught me to be successful."

We talked about the Redskins. "School is still out on them. There's more to a team than I can see in the pictures. I don't know what has been asked of them, so I don't know how much they've given. Most of all I don't know what they're like as men. You've got to make a choice between winning and losing."

He continued, "It's a funny thing in football that when a team has a weakness it always stays with them. There have been N.F.L. teams that could have been champions except that they lacked good offensive guards. They trade for them and they draft them, but year after year guards are always their weakness. And year after year they're losers."

I wondered if the priest in him was trying to sum up the Redskins in an oblique parable. Certainly, the Redskins have more than one notorious weakness. I tried to probe by name and position. He said he didn't want to deal in personalities.

We talked about success. Everyone in Green Bay had said, perhaps with the gift of hindsight, that they knew Lombardi was a winner the moment they laid eyes on him. I asked if he had had any doubts on that score, if he was apprehensive about taking over a dispirited ball team. "I've never been apprehensive in my life," he said. "You've got to do things according to your own personality and being apprehensive isn't part of mine."

I asked about a speech he had given to business groups several years ago in which he said the clamor for individual freedom had been twisted to mean a disrespect for authority. He had said that ninety-five percent of men wanted to be led rather than to lead, and that the call for too much freedom would cut these people adrift from the stability and values they needed to survive. It was a thesis that had been developed with the usual Lombardi intensity, the flat assertions of black and white, the noticeable absence of even the slightest apprehension.

Long hair doesn't mean anything," Lombardi said. "It may be dirty looking and I may not like it, but it doesn't mean anything.

But I am disturbed at what's happening. This idea of running free-lance and doing what you please is not freedom, but license." Then he went on to say that because the old perceived what the young are doing purely as "license," they feared it and might seek to repress it with violence and brutality. It would be a terrible failure, he said, "a sign that they couldn't communicate, because the kids and the discontented have something important to say."

We talked about poverty and racial tensions. "We are our brother's keeper, I don't give a damn what people say," he said. "If people can't find work, whether it's their fault or not, you've got to help them, clothe them, and house them properly and try to get rid of the conditions that have held them back." He said he is an inte-grationist, that the problem with black separatism is that black peo-ple are not separate and independent. Like everyone else they are dependent on others, they need the strength and size of a whole community. "Any kind of separatism is bad," he said, "in football or anywhere else." I asked if he found it disquieting that there was a dichotomy between his public image and his private views, that he was in political accord with many who scoff at him, while many who profess to find him a political prophet hold views he must regard as repugnant. He gave a faint affirmative twist of the hand. Or so I thought. In any event he smiled.

We turned to Green Bay and loyalty. Don't forget," he said, "I was everything out there when I was coach and general manager. I made a horrible mistake when I stepped out of coaching, but to go back to it in Green Bay would have hurt people."

"Bengtson?" I asked.

"Him particularly. If I were coaching and someone else in the organization were questioning me, I couldn't take it. I could never do that to anyone else. So it's not true that I was disloyal to Green Bay. I think there is always a time when a man who has contributed his life and efforts to whatever should be a part of that whatever. And that's why I came to Washington."

He talked about Paul Hornung. "I don't care how I personally come out in Green Bay. I was concerned with the Packers. I don't care whether they say I'm a snob or not in Green Bay, but if some-one said anything against Paul or the Packers I'd fight that man. I don't know why Paul was the type of pressure player he was. Maybe it was because he knew the tougher the situation the more glory there was for him in it. Inside the twenty-yard line Paul was the greatest player I've ever seen, just average downfield, but inside the twenty, the greatest."

What can I in turn say about Lombardi? He is a man who believes in himself. There was the seminary training, the priest-teachers at Fordham, the eight years in the parochial high school, West Point. They added up to thirty years in an ivory tower where doubts did not flourish, where there was the wrong way to do things and the Church's way, the wrong way to do things and the Army's way. These were years spent in the company of children, oversized waifs of one sort or another who needed the guiding hand of discipline, regularity, order. It was not the most broadening environment. Yet clearly Lombardi has transcended it, keeping what is essential in it to quiet his own insecurities, to still the doubts of others.

At bottom, the Lombardi code of excellence is a distillation of those thirty years in the company of children, priests and soldiers. But it is a distillation with the added mix of Lombardi himself — larger, subtler, more restless, more complex in a Shakespearean sense than the narrow bounds of the code, the simplistic rules of loyalty and winning. He is not blind to the fact that life is a larger proposition than is taught at Fordham, at St. Cecilia Prep, at West Point, even in the Packer dressing room. Though he demands that others stay within the limits of the code, he himself will venture beyond it, will push himself to test the outer limits. He has described himself as a "conservative" coach. This is true of the "fundamentals" style of football the Packers played and the Redskins will play, but it is not true of Lombardi. He is in fact, a gambler, a risk-taker, a man willing to pit himself and his system against the long odds of the 1959 Packers and the 1969 Redskins. It is the gambler in him, the visionary, that gives him the capacity to lead men, to demand 110 percent with a straight face, to even inspire a sort of grim affection among his players. "Ask Coach if he's got room for an over-the-hill tackle," Henry Jordan said with a laugh when we parted in Green Bay. Jerry Kramer, now rich beyond the dreams of avarice, told newsmen in June that he would come out of retirement for a chance to play under Lombardi in Washington.

I had gone to Green Bay prepared to find some holes in the Lombardi code. They were there all right. But I also think I found a man who is daring, who is struggling against his doubts.

Perhaps like Hornung he is a man who seeks risks and pressure because there is greater personal glory in it. At midfield Lombardi is often mediocre, selfish, inconsistent, sometimes even outrageously absurd, but within the twenty-yard line he has greatness. He does the important things well, the things he sets out to do, and he does them with incontestable drama.

24

A Season with Lombardi
by Tom Dowling

On Tuesday morning, he began all over again for a game that meant nothing, a game that ended a season that had no discernible scope for further achievement. What could you say about that Dallas game? To win it would be nice, 8-4-2. To lose it unpleasant, but endurable, 7-5-2.

Lombardi buttered himself a piece of toast and poured a cup of coffee. It was about 8:20 Tuesday morning. He had arrived at the stadium a few minutes before, had hung his suit coat and shirt in his locker stall, and was puttering about, getting himself ready for the day, coming to terms with the week that still lay ahead.

"I'm tired, bone tired," he told me. "Let me tell you, this has been a long season. They're all long, I guess. Maybe I'm getting older, but this one has seemed longer."

"What will this week be like?" I asked.

"Same as the others," he muttered. "We stayed down at the office late last night diagramming Dallas' movies, getting that part out of the way. We got volumes of notes, reams of them. Now this afternoon and tonight we'll review the pictures again, defensively and offensively, all of the staff together. Dallas is always tough because they throw a lot of formations at you, do a lot of unusual stuff from week to week. Ordinarily, you'd be able to get down to drawing up the game plan earlier on Tuesdays than we've done so far. Ordinarily, I wouldn't take the team outside on Tuesdays. At Green Bay I let them watch the pictures and go home. But since this is my first year here, I want to do some extra coaching that I wouldn't ordinarily do. I've got to try new things and I don't know yet whether this team can handle them or not. Even after twenty some-odd weeks I still don't know the personnel. I've got to see more of these people to really know what they can do. So I've deliberately tried to give this team a crash course in my system. And maybe I've gone too far sometimes and that's why they've made so damn many errors in the game. But, what the hell, I think that's the way it had to be done.

"This afternoon we'll go back to the office and review the films again. We got to get that game plan done tonight to pass out tomorrow, even if we got to stay there all night long. Some of these teams are tough to dope out personnel-wise and sometimes you just don't come up with a key. You can look at the pictures and look at them and get nowhere. Sometimes there's nothing there, they're not doing anything, and you're trying to find something that's not there. Some nights you're lacking inspiration. You just sit there and sit there and nothing comes. And you got to sit until it does, because Wednesday morning the team's got to have every play diagrammed against every enemy defense and vice versa. One week we may block an odd man line one way and one week another. We got to make some judgment on their personnel and their defenses to their personnel and their defenses to figure out which. And if you make the wrong judgment you're in trouble.

You'd think it would get easier when you've been at it as long as I have, but it doesn't. It gets harder staying fresh, harder disciplining yourself to take the hours, the exhaustion. Harder this year because of not knowing the people. This year we've been too pressed to check over what we're doing on computers to make sure we're not repeating ourselves too much, not giving away a pattern other teams can diagnose.

"I don't think we are; we're aware of the problem, but I'd like to be even more certain. You can't have your people do the same thing week after week, make the same moves, block the same way. That means you've got to put a burden on your players to change, to vary themselves, and there are people who can't master those changes.

"I don't think my system is particularly complex. Just a question of basic intelligence, really. Some teams even give intelligence tests. I don't believe in them, because I'm a great believer in pounding it in hard enough so even a guy below normal can catch on. And, hell, catching on isn't a question of intelligence, really. You've always got slow learners and intelligent people who are so used to another system it's become a habit to them.

"That's why I've always said the biggest challenge in coaching is getting belief, getting people to believe in what you're telling them.

"At Green Bay I had younger people. That was fortunate. They weren't formed. They were willing to believe. And, hell, I make mistakes. I'm not always right, but as long as I'm coaching, my people have got to believe in what I'm teaching. You need that."

"Maybe it's the times that are different, makes it harder for players to adjust to you," I said.

He took his coffee and sat down in the wooden chair from which he lectured the press after home games. He stirred his coffee for a while.

"Yes, great changes have taken place in the country in the last ten years. It's the nature of the times that there's more tendency to question now than there was ten years ago. The father complex is not around anymore. Yet there are other ways to motivate people, too. People want to excel, that's a human constant. And a young man, because of his body, can excel in sports. That's the reason you can get kids to drive themselves into the ground to play this sport, to go out and play hurt. I've always thought the best football player is the one who loves the glory. Like Paul Hornung. A super glory player. Anytime you got inside the 20-yard line, anytime you got down near the goal line you gave the ball to Paul, because he'd get it in there somehow. Whether there was no blocking, or whatever the hell happened, he was going to get it in there. Anytime it was an ordinary game, Paul was an ordinary football player; the bigger the game the more extraordinary he became. I could sense that in him."

He stopped and stared me in the eye, as if to let the force of those remarks sink in. But that was not what he was thinking about, not what was on his mind.

"I'll tell you," he said with sudden vehemence, "we had a complete breakdown in the second half against the Saints. I could see things were going wrong from the sidelines, but it wasn't until I saw the pictures that I could see how bad it was. Our key people were breaking down, blowing their assignment. What does this mean? I wish I knew. Did it just happen? Or is it a weakness under pressure? I'll have to find that out. And to me that Saints game was a pressure game. It meant a winning season. There are some games you must win. If you lose the first game of the season, let's say, you still got the season ahead of you. But if you lose the second game then that third game becomes a pressure game, *the* pressure game. Because you don't often lose three in a row in this league and go anywhere. Anytime you're playing for more than just a win you're playing a pressure game, whether you're trying to break out of a losing streak, whether it's for the championship, or whether you're playing for a winning season like against the Saints. It's a question of extra significance.

"They were asking me yesterday if the first Dallas game wasn't important. Well, hell yes, it was important. But it wasn't overwhelmingly significant. You could still see that the season wasn't over, that we could still be in the race if we lost to Dallas that first time. Yes, beating them meant facing pressure, but not absolutely. And the fact was we played a fine ballgame against Dallas. I've got to ask: Did we play that well because they didn't feel the pressure? You look at the New Orleans game, where the pressure is there, and you see them coming apart in the second half. Some people do things very well under pressure, some don't. I am at my best under pressure, I think. And I've been with teams that have won championships under pressure. I have to have some faith that being your best under pressure counts for something."

"How are you going to get them up for this last game?" I asked.

"I don't know. I just don't know yet. Something will come to me, I guess. It usually does." He looked at his watch. "In another hour I'll be on them, oh, won't I just," he laughed. "The films won't be much fun for anyone today. Then after I've told them what they've done wrong I'll have to wait, wait and see what their reaction is outside. I try to shut out everything negative about them after we've seen the films.

"As far as the tongue-lashing goes, it depends on what they're going to do on Wednesday and Thursday. How hard can you drive them? That's something that's got to come natural, something you've got to feel. Sometimes you don't have to say anything all week. They'll carry themselves. Sometimes you've got to whip them; well, drive them, I don't like the word whip."

"You don't like to think of yourself as a heartless man, do you?" I said, the season close enough to the end so that risks in being blunt had vanished.

"No. Why would anybody? It's no damn fun being hard. I've been doing this for years and years and years. It's never been great fun. You have to drive yourself constantly. I don't enjoy it. It takes a hell of a lot out of me. And, Christ, you get kind of embarrassed with yourself sometimes. You berate somebody and you feel disgusted with yourself for doing it, for being in a job where you have to. Fortunately, I don't remember. They say this is a game where you should have a memory like an elephant. Me? I try to forget. I've learned that when you forget certain things it's easy to keep going ahead. I yell and then I come back in here and it's all wiped out."

"But not necessarily for the people you've yelled at."

"No. But this is a game of survival. You've got to learn to survive yourself. I hope, I think they'll come to understand that whatever I've said is not going to carry. Not next week or two weeks from now, not even tomorrow. I'll judge them fresh from what I see tomorrow, not from what I remember from today. Of course, the time may come with a man that he does the same thing wrong day in and day out. That's a different proposition. You can't forget that."

"Will you let up on a guy if you've been on him too hard?"

"Never. No carrot and stick for me. I'll never look for a way to make it up to a guy I've been on. That doesn't mean I won't push some people more than others. You've seen me on the field and there are obviously people I push all the time and some I don't. There are many people here it took me a longer time to find out how far I could push and I don't know yet what their limit is. I'll be pushing them all over again next year until I do find their limit. By the same token, there are some people I knew I couldn't push. Some people I had doubts about and I pushed them and berated them to find out what I could about their character, their limits. Those are the things that are important to me, because this is what the game of football is really all about."

"How about the color question?" I asked.

"I've always had good relationships with black players. I like to think the reason is I don't know they're black. Everybody is the same damn color. When I'm mad at them and when I'm not. Now racial prejudice is one of the few areas where we've got a bad record as a nation. As far as football, it's been there. No getting around it. It's hurt teams. It can destroy them. I'm not saying I don't know who's black and who's white on this club. I'm just saying that I have no sense of it when I'm dealing with my people. The Negro ballplayers in this society have got a pretty good sense of people with color consciousness, for knowing when you're treating them differently from whites, either bending over to be nice or to be critical. Even when a coach doesn't intend to see black people as black people it shows. You can't hide it if you feel that way. I don't feel that way. I'm grateful for that, because first of all to feel that way is wrong, and second, it's good football not to feel that way.

"Well," he said with a benign smile, "I guess it's time to get ready to look at some movies." He walked in the little cubicle with the locker stalls, climbed out of his pants and T-shirt, and put on the thermal underwear, flannel knickers, and sweat shirt of his profession.

On Wednesday morning he buttered another piece of toast, poured a cup of coffee, and began browsing through the sports page of *The New York Times.*

"I thought you don't read the papers?" I said.

"I don't," he said still reading the *Times.* "I read the *Post* coming in in the limousine this morning. Normally I don't."

"In *Run To Daylight,* every chapter began with you stopping off to pick up the papers before you had breakfast at the drugstore," I said.

"That was early in my career. When I had some faith in what the papers said."

I laughed at that.

He said, "The problem with sportswriting now is they're writing about personalities instead of football. You can't blame them. The trouble is television. They're competing and television beats them to the punch, so the papers have to do something different, and as a result they don't give a damn what they do to people. If I do something wrong everybody's got to read about it. If I yell on the sidelines they got to write it up. That grates at me sometimes. Why not?"

I asked him if he found his return to coaching as satisfying as he thought it would be during that year of rustication in the Green Bay front office. He ignored the question and buttered another piece of toast. I repeated it.

"Satisfying? I don't know. You do what you have to do. I was unhappy out of coaching, let's put it that way. At first I though I wanted to do something different. I was asked to run for the Senate and the governorship."

"Did that tempt you?"

"I gave it some thought. I wasn't sure my nature was right for it. You know, I'm pretty sensitive to what they say about me in the sports pages. I wasn't sure I could take the beating you get in public life. At the same time I liked to think I could make a contribution to people. And then I was asked to go with a lot of big corporations and that tempted me, too. You like to think you can rise to a new challenge. But I wasn't sure about those things. For one thing I was under a tremendous amount of tension in Green Bay — three championship seasons in a row, twenty-two or twenty-three games a season, every game getting increasingly more tense. So I left to take a year's sabbatical, to get away from the tension and think. As it turned out a year was too long. Six months would have been plenty of time. Funny, I've always liked golf, always figured I could play a fair amount of it and be happy, but I found out quick enough that golf's not enough. And the more I played golf and sat in the office the more I realized I couldn't stay where I was.

"At first I thought it couldn't be coaching alone. Then I started to think, well, maybe I could get at least what I had in Green Bay. Then I started to think if I had the coaching, and the general manager's job and a piece of the club, well, that might be it. There were two things special I wanted: to be in the East and to be with a team I though I could reshape or re-do. Most of all, I guess I was sick to death of the publicity I was getting; the greatest coach ever, invincible, that sort of stuff. I felt I had to get back to the game. I'm just like anybody else. Nobody wants to be a legend, really. And you're no longer a legend once you come back, because then you're suffering defeats. You're getting beat. Not that I want to get beat, I'll tell you I don't. But I want to be alive, too, no dead legend.

"So it was great to be back. Hopefully, you can win, but, hell, the chances were small. I knew that. I knew a little something about the Redskins. The chances were small here. I want to tell you we got maybe five topflight football players. The ones in Green Bay who became topflight football players had the wherewithal to do it. They had something in them to get the job done. And I'm not too sure you can develop wherewithal.

"I did think so at one time. Maybe it was because of my ego, or whatever the hell I have, I thought I could develop it. I just don't know now. Maybe you need to start out with some inherent quality of excellence. The important thing is in having the spark in most, not just some, but most of your players. We've developed some of that spark here. But *some* is less than *most* and *most* is what you need for a championship."

"That's a pretty grim prognosis," I said.

"Well, you got to be grim to get there, you got to be grim to become a champion. Yet we've done some things here that are hopeful. Take injuries. Everybody talks about injuries; they say every team in the league has them. But we have less than most, maybe less than anybody.

"But at the same time *we don't really have less than anybody.* Our people have played with what injuries they have more than other teams have. It's very easy to say you're hurt and not perform. Now (Vince) Promuto is playing with big injuries. I'm not too sure he's doing the right thing. But I don't feel I should stop him. I like to develop that feeling of playing hurt. One hurt player teaches the others. That's worth it even if your injured player is not playing as well as he can, even if his play is hurting you a little bit. Because there's a question of leadership. You've got to have playing leaders. Now Sonny Jurgensen leads on the field. That's one of the best ways to lead. Sonny's the best athlete I have. I'm not so sure that he's interested in the personal glory the way Hornung was, yet he wants the team to win. He's got team pride, and team pride has always got to be larger than self-pride. Charley Taylor is the same way, he's getting that double coverage and he's not so upset about it. Charley has become a very disciplined player. Playing injured, personal glory, playing for the team to win, you need those things to go all the way. They create loyalty, and that can win some ballgames for you. Some of those tough ones you need to win on the days when you're not playing that well.''

"But wouldn't you say that team loyalty is something you don't have here the way you had in Green Bay?''

"Sure, it's much too early for loyalty. You can't talk about the Redskins in that way, not like you could with the Packers. And I didn't talk about loyalty in Green Bay until after the first year or so. You've got to have it, before you talk about it. I'm not going to get up and talk about loyalty if it's not there. This isn't a game where pretense works. You got to have it before you can talk about it. . . .''

By Thursday the lines of relief were etched on Lombardi's face. It was almost over, this six months of his life, and he wanted it to end, the weekly suspense to draw to a close.

"Have you figured out what you'll have to do to get them up for the Cowboys?'' I asked.

"They'll have to win this one for its own sake,'' he shrugged. "Some games you just have to play because they're on the schedule. No pressure. Just a game, and you got to learn to win the ones that are just there, the ones that don't have any big significance, too. In the end, that's how you get in the ones that count.

"Is it harder to prepare for Dallas with all their multiple offenses?'' I asked, mindful that the Cowboys' technological, explosive brand of football was said to be the wave of the future, while the Lombardi grind-out-the-yardage style was said to be passe. Mindful also of the fact that Morton has thrown the ball less than 300 times; Jurgensen more than 400. When it came to the stodgy offense Lombardi was not as culpable as the critics had it.

"When it comes to preparation, the difficulties are always with the teams you don't know, the teams in the other conference where you only play them once every two or three years,'' he said. "We know Dallas. The Redskins have played them two times a year. . . .''

On Friday, Lombardi was sprawled out in a wooden folding chair in the Coach's dressing room, with Christmas carols sounding dulcetly from the stereo speakers. He bent forward, pressing his palm to his back; a grimace passed his face. "I'm telling you, every time I sit down I get pains,'' Lombardi grumbled. "It's been a long time since I've had a day off, I want to tell you. The season doesn't bother you much, it's just every day, every day out there. It's the constant grind, you just wear out. Every other profession you get some time off, a Sunday or something. Monday, Saturday, I don't care, but some damn day or other. Even the players are so bushed they can't keep awake, and they're just youths."

One of the coaches looked up from a table where he was diagramming goal-line defenses. "Maybe we ought to flash a picture of a pretty girl up on the screen to keep them on their toes at the film sessions," he said.

"That's what we used to do in Green Bay," Lombardi reflected, his voice filled with respect for the sanctity of the past. "Flash one of those calendar babes up there on the screen, that ought to keep them awake. . . ."

It was bitter cold outside in the stadium that Friday morning. Plumes of vapor snorted from the mouth and nose of the players who climbed up the dugout steps onto the frozen R.F.K. Stadium turf for their last practice of the season.

Lombardi, for the first time that year that I had seen, led the team in its first exercise. He was swaddled like a bear in a greatcoat and his short arms and legs were barely visible as he did his jumping jacks, turning around in place, bestowing that huge, yet somehow shy and awkward grin of his on the whole team. There was no reason for the gesture to be touching, yet somehow it was. You could feel a certain electricity in the crisp winter air. It was, no doubt, the mood Lombardi sought; a sense of affectionate bondage would be the motivational key to Dallas. The team would play to win for Coach. Coach would coach to win for the team. They would be playing this one as a tribute to their season together.

On Saturday, as we all sat in the mobile lounge at Dulles Airport waiting to be driven and coupled to the Redskins' chartered jet, Lombardi spied a flamboyantly electric shirt on one of the players. "You guys are really something, you are," he sang out. And then grinning widely, looked from side to side for approval, he blushed. The team roared with laughter. "You guys are really something, you are, Mister," they all echoed with great pleasure. It seemed to me the Cowboys wouldn't have a prayer. . . .

The clock was ticking away and finally a time-out was called with three seconds on the board. Jurgensen unloaded another swing pass and went down, smothered for the last time by the Cowboy line . . . Dallas 20, Washington 10. The season was over. The two teams filed up the runway, the Cowboys smiling and chatting as they passed, their fans yelling down good wishes, an occasional Redskin trotting across the runway to pat a Cowboy on the rump and wish him luck against the Browns. Tom Landry came up the ramp, his face as blank and expressionless as a pan of dough. Then Lombardi passed by, his eyes narrow slits of smoldering anger, his lower jaw grinding away, an urgent bounce of revenge in his step.

He was, after all, the last of the poor losers. But, on the other hand, he was the last of the big winners. There were not many men who had won three of anything in a row in the 1960s. Lombardi had had occasion to do just that. He hadn't, after all, put his winning streak on the line for the hell of it. He cared so much about winning that he did not dissemble the ulcerous rage of defeat. And perhaps he had a point there. If men would not always play for the Spartan pride of glory, perhaps they would play out of the fear of a Spartan commander who made it simpler to face the prospects of victory than defeat.

The dressing room doors remained shut for some time. "What did he say?" I asked a player in the dressing room. "He said he was ashamed of us as men. He said the Cowboys didn't come out to win today and we showed we weren't men enough to teach them a lesson."

"He's got a point there. About the Cowboys at least," I said.

"Yeah, he does. Got something to say on the other point, too. You got to face that. We weren't any tigers out there today."

The reporters tracked Lombardi down in the hallway. Given the wind, why didn't he kick off instead of receiving the opening kick, he was asked.

"When you got a defense like ours you don't kick off. You take the football whenever you can. I didn't trust our defense, so the question of the wind didn't enter my calculations."

"Did you achieve what you set out to this year, Coach?"

"Somewhat."

"What did you and what didn't you?"

"That's for me to know."

The answer was obvious enough. The seven wins were what he set out to achieve. The five defeats and the two ties were what he didn't have in mind. That was what he hadn't set out to achieve.

So that was it: 7-5-2. That was what would finally stand up, all that would be remembered. In a matter off weeks the lethargy and shame of that final defeat against the Cowboys would be forgotten. It would be just another loss. So would the defensive breakdown against the Browns, the rout by the Colts triggered by a handful of errors, the loss of a victory on a doubtful clipping call in the first Dallas game, the closeness of defeat in the Rams game decided on a fumble and a defensive breakdown in the closing minutes. And the ties would look the same. The artistry of that final come-from-behind drive in San Francisco and the fiasco of the Eagle tie, achieved on an interference call on 4th and 25 — they both amounted to the same thing. The satisfaction of San Francisco merged with the self-loathing of Philadelphia. The wins — their characters so different — would ultimately seem the same. The Saints, the Cardinals, the Giants, the Steelers, the Falcons, the Eagles, the Saints again — they would all in the end merely add up to seven, lack any further individuality.

That was the nature of football. Only the final record would be remembered and on that scale the Redskins had barely tipped into respectability. You could forget the harshness of that code while the season was in progress, while you were aware of the injuries, the lack of depth, the lack of great overall talent, the unremitting pressure, the doubts and insecurities. But when it was all over these factors could no longer be conjured with. The numbers still came up 7-5-2, not good enough for the Division title. The code of football was winner take all. . . .

The Chiefs were the World Champions, not the Redskins, and the spoils went to Hank Stram, not Vince Lombardi. Lombardi accepted that. He was a poor loser, but he knew the code, did not seek the balm of illusion on that score. Indeed, he was a poor loser and a great coach precisely because he never lost sight of the harsh strictures of the code, because he was remorseless in the drive to win, secure in the knowledge that the only thing that would be remembered, that would count in the end, was the outcome of the Super Bowl. Second place, as he liked to say, was meaningless — second place in the Division, in the conference, in the League, and in the Super Bowl.

Anything short of total victory was unacceptable and the closer you got to the big game the more painful the denial of that final triumph. For the closer you came, the better football team you had, the more singleness of purpose you had shown over the long haul. The further you advanced in the playoffs the greater the crash of defeat, the more a player came to doubt himself and his team. . . .

The Redskins wanted to win all right, hungered for the glory, the money, the peace of mind that came with championships. But they hadn't done it before; they had some doubts about their ability to do it, worried about their own survival in the Lombardi scheme of things. In the end they had less talent, endured more pressure and fear that most teams, so their faith in winning was less and they cared less about the meaning of defeat.

Lombardi too had some doubts about their ability, was worried about his own survival in the Redskin scheme of things. Survival with him ran deeper than job security; it was championship survival that he worried about. But unlike the Redskins he had great faith in his ability to win; he cared about it totally and constantly. That faith was all that mattered, and like some primitive religion you could not tell where it would end, whether it would acquire the converts to thrive, but you knew it would endure, with or without your converts, that it would suffer in defeat but remain unchanged and immutable. Lombardi was the supreme loyalist — loyal to his code even if others were not prepared to embrace it.

The carpeted Cotton Bowl dressing room was littered with tape and soggy towels, the great red dufflebags were loaded into the bellies of the chartered buses for the last ride of the season. A motorcycle escort led the way onto the Dallas freeway, a courtesy for champions and Presidents. And the team deserved that. They were average football players perhaps, but they were a company of strong and honorable men. What team had faced greater pressure, worked harder, struggled longer with their own doubts and anxieties? They had played for a man who never yielded, who never accommodated, who never stopped driving them. They had almost broken, but in the end they had held, had come out on the winning side at 7-5-2, bloody perhaps, bowed as well, but not without a certain strength. Certainly, they could face the off-season, even July 1970 in Carlisle, Pa., with some measure of self-esteem.

For the first time in recent memory they had ended a season less diminished than they had begun it. . . .

I wandered up and down the aisle of the tourist section, saying goodbye to the players, knowing that I had only seen a small part of their lives, had only experienced a fraction of what they had gone though, had been up when their hopes were up, down when theirs were down, had wondered along with them if they would break or come through. It was not the same as knowing it for yourself, or feeling the exhilaration or despair of the action itself. But I had tried to get as close to it all as I could, had tried to see what it was like in the round. For me this flight home was the end of the line. There was no next season. The finality was there and I knew as much as I ever would. . . .

Frank Ryan asked, "What are you going to call your book?"

"I don't know yet."

"Well, if it's about football, tell what you know and call it *The Nature of the Beast.*"

"There's a double meaning there," I said.

"Oh my God yes, I forgot about that," he laughed.

The plane was nearing Washington and I went forward to the first-class section to beard the beast. Lombardi was sound asleep, an almost beatific smile on his face, the taut flesh of his grimacing lower face loose and relaxed, a stern Italian *pater familias,* a stone mason from the old country perhaps, a hewer of men down in the gridiron quarry, his job now finished, as good a piece of work as trying could make it, enjoying a little snooze, doubtlessly plotting the future already, just pausing briefly before the whole thing would begin all over again.

Later, I asked him to sum up the season. He said, "The greatest problem we had in training camp was the unknown. The biggest drawback was not knowing what they could do, trying to discover their limitations. Everyone has limitations. I do, the Packers did, this team does. You can't run away from them. You got to push and find them. So as a result I began this year groping, not knowing what I had, what I could demand. The first disappointment was the complete lack of running ability with the whole squad. I wanted to bury my face that first day when I saw them run. Just no runners. Oh, Charley Taylor could run, but not many others, I'm telling you. In our business you got to begin with overall running ability. You just can't win without it. Some of them had it and it was latent; they didn't know how to use it, didn't push themselves to bring it out.

"That was the first big limitation. The second one was how each and every one would react if they had the chance to win. Under pressure. There's not great pressure if you're a losing team, you know. You just go out there and win or lose, it doesn't make a damn bit of difference. So you win four ballgames or two or one, so what? But if you're a winning team, there comes the point when you find out about yourself, how you react to that pressure, how you react when the team you're going to play is ready for you.

"This is what we had to find out. Even the great performer that Sonny Jurgensen is, I couldn't answer what he was like under those circumstances. So it takes time away from the actual coaching to get at these questions, to find out where you stand, what kind of people you've got deep down.

"Then the next problem was my system. Coaching is two things; you got to be somewhat of a pedagogue, and at the same time you have to teach in such a way that the team has confidence in what you're saying. I had a great plus going for me there. No doubt about that. I had my past record, which helped a little bit, you might say. But at the same time it doesn't take very long in my business for that to go away. You can't say you're a winner just because you were one long ago. You're not a winner if you were a winner two or three seasons ago and you're losing ever since. You just don't fool people with that stuff.

"But this year I came with a certain reputation, a modicum of success behind me, you might say. And I have a personality that's made people believe in me. That helps. Still, the people you've got have got to, in the end, visibly see that my system works. Not someplace else, but right here. I think I have to say I am a teacher first and a coach second.

"The difference between teaching and coaching is selling yourself, being involved yourself right up to the neck. To be a teacher you got to win their hearts. Once you win a team's heart they'll follow you, they'll do anything for you. I haven't won their hearts yet, maybe. But it's not for lack of trying to. And I'll keep trying to. You can't just go out there and win and then go home and forget it. You got to go out there and live it all day long, be a part of it. You got to think all the time, in the car, at home, at night, looking at the pictures, out on the practice field. The thing that annoys me more than anything else is having a great ballplayer and not getting the performance from him he's able to give. I don't blame the ballplayer, I blame myself. I say something to that ballplayer. I yell at him, I scream at him, I go after him, I try to arouse him. And it's no damn fun, but I'm thinking to myself I've been a failure for this guy. I've got to reach him and I haven't. And because I hate being a failure more than anything else, I go to work on that man. I really go after him to reach him.

"I use a lot of cliches or whatever you want to call them and, fine, they may be cliches to other people, but they're not cliches to me. And I hope they're not cliches to the people I'm talking to. Because if they believe them the way I believe them we're a team, we're united, we can win. . . .

"We did end up a winner. And although that satisfied me, it was also good for the team. It broke this damn cycle of losing and that can make a difference to us. We're not a greatly talented team, but we're not losers, either. Not anymore. . . ."

"You finished this year 7-5, the same record you had your first year in Green Bay," I said. "Yet then at the end of '59 you must have known that the Packers were ready, were good enough to go all the way the next year. You don't have that same feeling about the '70 Redskins, I guess."

He made an indistinct sound in his throat, a sort of rasping acknowledgment that this was so. "The Packers were young and they were deep in talent. It was all there. You could see it, you could feel it. The Redskins? They're not that young, not that talented. But we'll be there, we'll be giving it what we've got. Hell, there's no other way."

Now the jet was nearing home. The lights of suburban Washington were flickering on the ground below us. The pressure was beginning to squeak in the eardrums. I got out of my seat. Lombardi, a man who always reacted to pressure, had just woken up, was stifling a yawn. The beast looked pretty tame, the flesh in his face softened and relaxed. It was as if the man he had been for the last six months was a creation of the imagination, an act of his own will. Now he looked to be a good-natured, short, middle-aged Italian-American with greying hair and a mouthful of big square teeth, but perhaps, too, a man who could be really something — he could, when he put his mind to it.

I thanked him for his kindnesses, for the enjoyment I'd had in these last months and the chance to learn what I had. . . .

Lombardi gave a weary smile, we shook hands, and I went back to my seat, as the plane dipped over Dulles.

In a few minutes the jet would land and the team would leave the terminal for the darkened parking lot. They would disappear, many of them to come back to play another day and many never to be heard of again. This was for them a homecoming and a diaspora. The 1969 Redskins were all over. In 1970 there would be new people, a new schedule, a new league, and in the end a new fate based on a new won-lost record. In 1970 it would begin all over again, all different, and probably all very much the same.

As a team they had done their best. I was not good enough, but it was better than they had ever done together, better than many thought them capable of. As men they had quality and character. As a team they lacked a soul, would never really be happy, able to win until they found the soul Lombardi wanted. There was no room for compromise on that score. The seeds of tragedy for all of them were still there.

Lombardi for his part had a soul, but he lacked a team. He had been the great winner, the champion of the sixties in a game that had no other standard of excellence, or even meaning, beyond winning. He had put it all back on the line and now he would enter the 1970s an underdog, a man just a shade over .500.

You had to admire that. The gall of it, the daring, the need to prove himself afresh. He was no fool, could size up the prospects of the 1969 Redskins as well as anyone. Better than anyone, perhaps. For he was by nature a pessimist, a realist, a man who never discounted the worst. Why had he done it, then? I had to believe that for all the doubts, the bleak assessments of what was and could not be altered, he was a man who believed in himself, and accordingly sought risks, and great odds to reaffirm that faith. . . .

So football was a profession that offered a man complete control, the knowledge he had done it himself. There had to be pride in that. And Lombardi was a man strongly moved by pride, by the sense that he alone was responsible and he alone had made it possible. Some pride was there at 7-5-2. The next step was glory, and he was a man who believed in that as well, had waited a long time for it to come in the pre-Green Bay days and was willing to wait and to push and push in Washington until it came again.

Once Lombardi had asked Paul Hornung whether he wanted to be a playboy or a football player. "Both," said Hornung and Coach was said to have laughed. On another occasion Hornung had climbed aboard the team bus prior to a game, his collar smeared with lipstick, his eyes a trifle red. "Where you been?" Lombardi grunted. "To church," Hornung answered in a dulled voice. "To church, to church, he's been to church," Lombardi chuckled to himself all the way to the stadium, rocking back and forth in his seat at the head of the bus.

That was glory to Lombardi, the merger of these two worlds: playboydom and football, the church and a night on the town, the saint and the sinner. That was why Paul Hornung was for him *the* football player, the only one I had ever heard him mention with something like the total approval and happiness of beatitude. . . .

Perhaps he was the man that Lombardi longed to be, "The Golden Boy," not just one of "The Seven Blocks of Granite." Hornung had tasted the rewards, here and now, that Lombardi had waited these long, long twenty-five years of apprenticeship to get. Hornung had had the glory and the pleasure young; it had come easy to him, had arrived without the need of discipline. To Lombardi it had come late in life. He was forty-five when the big break came, when he got a team of his own. Those years of obscurity must have grated, the dreariness, the moritification of being someone else's assistant. The price of discipline must have cost him. But he had suffered it, and, as he liked to say, he was willing to pay the price.

When I had first met Lombardi, back in May, he had told me of Hornung, "I don't know why Paul was the type of pressure player he was. Maybe it was because he knew the tougher the situation the more glory there was for him in it. Inside the twenty-yard line, Paul was the greatest player I've ever seen; just average downfield, but inside the twenty the greatest."

Lombardi clearly had that quality. Perhaps like Hornung he sought risks and pressure because there was greater personal glory in it. At midfield Lombardi was harsh, merciless, egoistic, inconsistent, often even mediocre, but within the twenty-yard line he had greatness. He did what he had to do. For him, unlike Hornung, it was not easy. It was an extraordinary act of will, of discipline, of ceaseless driving. The yardage inside the twenty was always tough. For Lombardi it was tougher than for most and he never flinched, just kept pushing. Hell, there was no other way.

25

Invincible Vince
by Jerry Izenberg

Once, a long time ago, Vince Lombardi walked the sidelines of a small New Jersey ball park and gazed grimly at the field where his St. Cecilia High School team was about to have the state's longest winning streak shattered. He seemed to grow smaller and smaller. It did not matter to him that he had dominated his opposition for so long. What mattered was that he was about to lose a football game, and nowhere since they began playing the sport has there been a harder loser than Vincent T. Lombardi.

As a matter of fact, when he had come to Green Bay in 1959, he had brought with him a peculiar legacy. Nowhere, as a player at Fordham, as head coach in high school, as an assistant coach in college and with the Giants, had Vince Lombardi ever experienced a losing season. But when he arrived from the East with his family, he had stepped into what had become one of pro football's graveyards. The Packers, reorganized after near-bankruptcy, were in the midst of total failure.

In 1959, his first year as coach, he gave them respectability. A year later he had them in the title game, forcing the Eagles to the limit before losing, and now here he was back again against the Giants. He might not be a magician, people around Green Bay conceded, and then again he might be.

Who were these Packers whom Lombardi had made into football's most feared professional team, and how was it done? "You do not join the Green Bay Packers," his players were fond of saying, "you enlist." From the moment he assembled the squad at pre-season camp at nearby St. Norbert's College that year, it was apparent that here was a man who was as spartan in his own preparations as he expected his players to be in theirs.

This was a team put together with infinite care. Bart Starr, the quarterback, couldn't throw like Unitas and couldn't scramble like Otto Graham. "All he can do," Lombardi liked to say, "is beat you." Paul Hornung had been a quarterback at Notre Dame and had languished on the Packer bench under the previous regime. Lombardi made him a halfback, thereby utilizing Hornung's talents as both runner and thrower. Moreover, Hornung could and did placekick.

There were so many others: Ray Nitschke, a savage linebacker who broke training and won ball games; Willie Wood, a superb defensive back who had to beg for a tryout. There was Jimmy Taylor, the powerful fullback out of L.S.U. who combined with Hornung to give Green Bay the best inside-outside combination in the league. And behind it all was the guiding hand of Lombardi, who wheeled and dealed and traded and put all the pieces together.

Their title game opponents, the Giants, were playing their first season under a bright new young coach named Allie Sherman. Eleventh-hour trades on the eve of the season had brought the Giants a venerable quarterback named Y. A. Tittle and a skinny pass receiver named Del Shofner. Together they led New York to the Eastern title.

Now they were to meet in Green Bay, and on the Tuesday preceding the game the temperature plummeted to 12 below zero. The wind charged down Green Bay's narrow streets. It was, natives claimed, perfect football weather. The Giants arrived on Thursday, and by the time their plane landed, the weather had warmed to a balmy 15 degrees. All of Green Bay was in an uproar. There had never been a title game in town before. Visitors rolled over in their hotel beds to answer the phone and heard the desk clerk say, "Howdy, Packer-Backer. It's eight o'clock." The Giants had Tittle, but Green Bay was confident. Green Bay had Vince.

And Green Bay had something else too. Both Hornung and Nitschke had been called to serve with reserve Army units. By special dispensation, they would be granted leave from their duties to play in the title game.

Rarely, if ever, has a championship game produced so little competition. "The Giants were more concerned about the weather than anything else," Bill Forester, a Green Bay linebacker, later explained. "They came with tennis shoes, gloves and scarves. We just came to play."

The pattern upon which Green Bay would depend became evident at the start. Lombardi sent his linebackers swarming over Tittle, who was having even more trouble avoiding Willie Davis, the Packers' bruising defensive end. When the game ended, Tittle had completed only six of 20 passes against the suicide defense. The Giants, meanwhile, had gambled everything on halting the powerful inside rushing of Taylor. Over this bruising spectacle loomed the large and effective figure of Paul Hornung, boy soldier.

He scored 19 points — six with his feet and 13 with his toe — a new individual championship scoring mark. He got the first one with a six-yard run at the start of the second period, and in the gray Green Bay twilight he concluded the afternoon's scoring with a 19-yard field goal. In between these efforts, he dominated the contest. At the finish it was Green Bay 37, New York 0.

White-helmeted members of Green Bay's Civilian Defense Corps cleared a path for the players to the dressing rooms just back of the park. Lombardi stood off in a corner and said over and over, "There has never been a better team than this one was today."

The only printable quote from the other side was heard as reporters raced into the silent Giants' locker room. A muddy, weary Giant, who did not have to be reminded of the final score, looked up and simply said, "Shut the damn door."

It was December 31, 1961, and they still talk about the kind of New Year's Eve they had that year in Green Bay.

26

Why He Was a Winner
by Jerry Izenberg

The legend will grow. Conceived in fact, it will draw on the memories of too many people who will insist they were there. Caesar dangles a Patrician toe in the Rubicon and simpers "you know my togas fade when they're damp" and it comes up "the die is cast." A jerk with a bugle has only learned one call and The Light Brigade comes on like it really knew where it was going.

And in Green Bay, Wis., a man coaches a football team and wins... and wins... and suddenly he is not a coach at all. He is a Prussian drillmaster. He is Attila sweeping through Chalot. He is John Henry with his hammer in his hand, beating the rest of football to a bloody pulp through brute stength, extra-sensory perception and a diet of honey and wheat germ.

This is the way it is because Vincent Lombardi has left his last coaching footprints in the snows of the Everest which is professional football in America today. This is the way it is because he wrapped up his third-straight National Football League title in 1967 and nobody else has ever done that. This is the way it is because he won the first two Super Bowls, one more than everybody else. This is the way it is because he rescued people like Henry Jordan and Willie Davis and Willie Wood from obscurity.

Like hell it is.

There are qualities which made Vince Lombardi a winner and

they are neither mystical nor un-nameable. Winners terrify people. Pro football itself is a winner in our society today and instead of asking "did he catch it or drop it?" people watch the guards in search of some mystical Rosetta Stone. Vincent Lombardi was a winning coach and every time they put him under the microscope, they picked up a pair of field glasses and tried to pinpoint him by looking through the wrong end.

So the Lombardi legend belongs to the future. . . to the amateur psychologists. This is simply about the way it was, starting with the day in 1959 when Vincent Lombardi — then 46 years old and with a high-school job as his only previous head-coaching experience — sent his first Packer team out to meet the world, and zeroing in on the 1967 team that put the final punctuation to it all.

"It's the team," Lombardi says of the winning tradition he built. "It's the team as a unit." The first time you hear it, you say this is either corn or con. "Come on, Vincent. This is pro football not the Rover Boys at Harvard." The second time you hear it, you are not so sure. The more you hear it, the more you wonder.

As guard Jerry Kramer, who was there in '59, says: "You sit there and you listen and in the beginning you don't believe it. He stands up and he says that football players are a dime a dozen and you nod your head up and down and all the while you are saying 'bull, bull, bull.' Then he says, 'Men with more talent than you have sat in this room but they're not here now,' and you nod again and you say 'bull, bull, bull.' And then he says, 'You're here because you make this team what it is. You're here because all of you fit.' And then one day you stop nodding. . . because you know it's the way it really is."

When you don't fit, you don't stay. One day Jim Ringo goes to the mat hard over salary negotiations. Jim Ringo gets traded. It costs him maybe $40,000 over the long haul, but on a hot summer night in Cincinnati, Jim Ringo is thinking not about money but about how it was in Green Bay under Vincent Lombardi. He is watching the New York Jets file by for their pre-game warm-up at a meaningless exhibition game.

They are football players like all football players. And then the one in the white shoes trots by. His name is Joe Namath, and Jim Ringo smiles and says in much the same way a draftsman views a Renoir: "Boy, I'd like to see the kind of football player he'd be if

Lombardi had five minutes alone with him."

It is the voice of a professional far from home. Despite the acrimony which marked the trade that sent him off to Philadelphia, it makes clear that Jim Ringo feels very keenly that Vincent Lombardi is still a very special kind of football coach.

But still you wonder: Why do they let him run them the way he does? You hear the players talk about fear and you want to laugh. You think of these men who can break arms and crack ribs in their world of giants and you think of a man half their size and it seems so ridiculous. But the fear is there. It lives and breathes and it works. But it is a different kind of fear. Before the legend runs its course let Willie Davis tell it the way it really is:

"The idea of the team," Willie says, stretching out his stocking feet and filling the bed in a room at Green Bay's The Northland Hotel on the eve of the N.F.L. title game with Dallas, "the idea of a team is real. You believe it because it works. Now, he picks his people. He picks them on ability and he picks them on something else. He knows us. And the fear is so simple. It's just the plain, frightening idea that something will prevent you from remaining a part of this."

"Something?" a vistor asked.

"Okay," Willie said, grinning, "someone."

Years from now, they will say that Vincent Lombardi revolutionized football and they will be wrong about that, too. They will look back at the type in the record books and this will confirm their beliefs that he brought new techniques to this game, and they will say that 1967 must have been the climactic year in his revolution and they will be right about this. . . but for all the wrong reasons.

The team which Vince Lombardi took to the third title (or which took him, if you listen to his critics) came into the season torn and bleeding. Its quarterback, Bart Starr, was a mass of bruises. Its offense attacked the giants around it with all the vigor of a ruptured paramecium. There was nothing complicated about what was wrong with the Packers. You simply cannot win with a wounded quarterback.

But they did. The Packer defense moved in and picked it up until Starr recovered. Then they came into New York. And in the second half, the Packers tore three-lane highways in the Giants' defense. Okay, nothing special about that last season. But the offense was something else, and afterward there was offensive halfback Elijah Pitts, who was dressed in nothing but a smile in the Packer locker room, saying:

"You know, every time the ball turns over and we go off and the defense comes in we yell things at each other. It was getting embarrassing. We were so bad we had reached the point where we couldn't think of anything to say."

Now legend will go on to prove that Vincent Lombardi was a holy terror over that stretch. He believes in pushing his people, which, in truth, is why he won so many games. "I'm hard on them," Vince Lombardi once admitted to a co-worker at a league meeting in one of the two great understatements of the century. "Some of them can't take it. If they can't, they can't do it for me."

But except for the minor adjustments — the pure football changes which every coach, winner or loser, feels compelled to make — the coach never pushed the panic button. There were enough reasons to do so if he had been so inclined.

He could read the papers and they would tell him that the team was old and tired and ready to be taken. He could think about that third-straight title, the one they said nobody could win. Or he could think about the firm, secret decision he had already made and which ticked away inside him like a bomb in search of a fuse.

He was going to step down as coach and this was going to be the year. He had tipped it almost casually to some of the more perceptive members of the offensive unit the previous January 1967, before the Super Bowl in Los Angeles. At a meeting in the team's Santa Barbara training camp he had said:

"This is not the most important game of my career. Next year at this time, it might be."

And from the moment the Packers went to camp there were players who were watching and waiting and wondering. In devious ways they tried to pry the secret loose.

"Coach is going to be like George Halas," Jerry Kramer said to Marie Lombardi one day. "He's just going to go on forever."

"Like heck he is," Mrs. Lombardi replied.

"I would have done it a year sooner," Lombardi told a man two days after he announced his formal retirement as coach in 1968. "I would have done it last year except we had the Taylor thing and then there was so much rebuilding to do with expansion I just felt I needed this year.''

The problems of which Lombardi spoke were, indeed, serious enough to delay his timetable. Despite his evangelical zeal about "the team...the team...the team"...the barrel over which his fullback, Jim Taylor, had placed him by playing out his option, treatened to test this team theory to the utmost. And Lombardi intended to remain as the man with the whistle while the testing was being done.

Taylor and Paul Hornung had been the Packers' bread-and-butter runners ever since Lombardi took over the team. In 1966, it was obvious that neither would return the following season. Fullback, of course, was the big problem. Lombardi was left with a relatively untested bonus baby named Jim Grabowski at the position. It was, once again, necessary for the theory of "the team is bigger than any man" to stand up. Vince chose to keep the responsibility on his own shoulders. As things developed, he found three fullbacks to bail him out at various times...Grabowski, then Ben Wilson, who came over after an undistinguished career with the Rams, and a New York Giants' castoff named Chuck Mercein.

Expansion had brought the New Orleans club into existence and Green Bay had to make players available to it. In addition, age was creeping up on several key veterans, including guard Fuzzy Thurston and end Max McGee. And there were other men of whom Lombardi was unsure. Rebuilding, in the sense Lombardi spoke of, meant developing kids named Flanigan, Hyland, Williams and Gillingham. It meant testing the Andersons and the Grabowskis. It meant building a solid club to leave behind for Phil Bengtson, an aide whom he had already mentally chosen as his own replacement. So much for the motives behind his thinking in 1966.

And this is why 1967 was, indeed, climactic in terms of Vincent Lombardi's fantastic run through the National Football League. He was tough as hell. He was pure sulphuric acid at the game-film sessions each Tuesday. But he is always that way. He reached down and drew his inside straight right out of the very depth of the system he has lived by ever since he came to Green Bay. Torn and bleeding at the midpoint, the Packers were running flat out at the finish when they won the ones they had to win. They simply played his game.

"It's emotion," Lombardi said, sitting behind his big, wide desk in the lushly carpeted second-floor office of the building he helped make possible. "It's at least 75 percent emotional, and this has been a very emotional season."

This was on the eve of the Dallas game on a day when Green Bay, Wis., had all the charm of a week behind a dog sled, and the only emotion a visitor could conjure up in his mind was the fear at what degree the human eyeball will freeze.

"A coach has to be careful how much you can force them to be ready.

"You mean you could leave your season out on the practice field?"

"No, I mean you could lose halfway through the schedule."

So in its way it is a con game. It is a question of finding the right words at the right time. There is nothing wrong with this. Salesmen, politicians and generals all live by the same rules. The trick is to know that the troops can back it up once you convince them.

And the season goes like this. Before the regular-season game against the Rams — at a time when the Packers had already clinched their divisional title — he stands up and tells them that the league is depending on them to play their best game. Even Rockne wouldn't have had the nerve to tell Notre Dame to win one for Pete Rozelle. A bad guess, you think?

Then consider this. Consider that despite all the talk about what Deacon Jones did that afternoon — and he was magnificent despite the talk in the Rams' dressing room about destiny, the Rams of Los Angeles, who were fighting for their lives, beat the Packers of Green Bay on the strength of a blocked kick in the final seconds. If Lombardi had only had a George Gipp instead of Pete Rozelle going for him, he might have made it.

Then of course, as you recall, the Packers finish by losing to Pittsburgh. It is a natural letdown. The team looks ahead to the Western playoff with the Rams, but because it knows its coach it is sullen and uneasy and a little afraid. It believes that somehow there is a master plot afoot. Later that night a Packer player says, "That so-and-so wanted to hang something on us for next week." The club considers itself properly hanged.

The Rams come to Milwaukee, that separate but nearly equal lair of the bear, and the coach walks into the Packer locker room and says "This is the most important game of your life." They win it big.

Now it is Dallas and the N.F.L. title is at stake and this time it is Green Bay and the kind of eyeball-splitting cold which makes Forrest Gregg, the big offensive tackle, grin and think about his native Texas and say, "Weather? Don't worry, they'll worry about it. This is the only time in my life when I'm happy I'm a lineman."

Lombardi walks into the dressing room. He tells them (all right, so you guessed it): "This is the most important game of your life." Again they win it. In January, Doug Hart, a reserve defensive back, sits near the pool at a luxury motel in Florida as the Super Bowl countdown begins. "For two-straight games he's told me it's the most important game of my life, and the hell of it is that for two-straight games he's been right and I know it."

It sounds so easy. It happens on college campuses all over the country every week. But Green Bay, Wis., is not a college campus. The athletes who work out of there are professionals. Without the other pieces, none of this works. The other pieces were always there. That's because Vincent Lombardi began putting them there right from the start.

Finding Willie Wood for a postage stamp, rescuing Willie Davis and Henry Jordan from limbo, picking the niche for Paul Hornung — all of these and the 30 or so other stories that go with them are history. They belong to the legend-makers.

The first thing that does not belong to the legend-makers is the plain, startling fact that all of this almost never happened. In 1957, just one year before Green Bay made its initial contact with Lombardi, he was serving as offensive coach with the Giants under Jim Lee Howell. Down in Philadelphia, Hugh Devore was finishing the last of two dismal seasons as head coach of the Eagles. Hughie was on his way out. Though few people know it, the Eagles wanted Lombardi.

The offer came and it was an enormous temptation. After all, Vincent Lombardi had been at his trade for some time by then. He had been a head coach at St. Cecilia High School in Englewood, N.J. He had returned to his alma mater at Fordham as an assistant. From there he had moved up to West Point, again as an assistant, under Red Blaik.

West Point, that was supposed to be the place. Col. Blaik hired well and all of college football knew it. The Colonel hired them and trained them and then, like a giant revolving door, he sent them spinning off to all parts of the country to fill head-coaching vacancies. But Vince Lombardi didn't get one. At age 41, he moved back down the Hudson to take the offensive coaching job with the Giants.

Nobody can look inside a man — except the legend-makers — and so nobody will ever know what Vince Lombardi felt through those years. But surely the fire did not suddenly burst into flame in Green Bay. Surely it was there all along. A man who watched him coach as an assistant at Fordham recalls he was "something of a wildman. He was so intense that he wanted to put people into the game who were already in it."

And at West Point, there was a day when he threw his baseball cap on the ground in a fit of rage and he and Col. Blaik had a long talk. The legend-makers would have you believe that this is unique but you can see it on every football field. You don't have to catch the pros either. Try Tuscaloosa, Ala., or Columbus, Ohio, for openers. If you want to win, you drive yourself and everyone around you. There is a large dent in the wall where this is being written because a man threw an Olivetti portable typewriter at it one night. Look in the mirror the next time the boss' nephew gets the raise instead of you.

So the drive to strike out on his own was there — and even his most fervent critics concede that he put it to work at Green Bay as no other pro coach had ever been able to put it to work before him. The drive and other things, too.

The toughness which Vince Lombardi has generated throughout his brief but incredible dynasty rubs off in a strange way. Publicly, Vince Lombardi takes no particular pride out of his personal toughness. He prizes it as a necessary ingredient in his route. When you get down to it, you can detect a strange kind of pride in the players' attitudes about Lombardi's use of that quality.,

So in the end it all comes back to that wonderful, sophomoric cliche "the team." But it's there, baby, and it is what this Green Bay franchise as been all about ever since Vincent Lombardi took charge of it.

"It's human beings," the coach says. "There's no real place in actual coaching for an I.B.M. machine." Vince Lombardi had, indeed, brought the computer to pro football. He housed it on the same floor as his private office. He hired a staff to feed it and clothe it and keep its nose clean. He used it for everything from helping to select draft choices (it came up with a kid named Travis Williams) to revealing facts about every player on every team the Packers would ever oppose. Once, with a genuine grin split across his face, he told the visitor: "The machine says that anybody with more than a 130 I.Q. won't hit."

He claims that the quality he sought could not actually be put into words. A man suspects that he claims this because the only words that fit do come up as cliche. . . words like pride and courage and sacrifice. They come straight out of Frank Merriwell but they are the touchstones of the Lombardi system. He may not want to name them but he knows how to find them.

"Well, you happen to be the man who put it in."

"Yes, but not to coach. It's emotions. There are certain people you want and certain people you don't and I'm not only speaking about talent."

The theory is that Lombardi tested them — every single day of his tenure as coach. In the beginning, he tested them on the kickoff squad. Some other places, you have a warm body, you put him on this unit until you figure out what to do with him. In Green Bay, it is different. The theory is that Lombardi tests them then and there for courage. It does not take long to find out.

Injuries? They play with them. The veterans will tell you that this, too, is part of the test.

Discipline? Take it back to the Plains of West Point and Col. Blaik. There was no time for humor in Earl Blaik's football. There is no time for humor in Vincent Lombardi's football.

There is a great mystique about pro football, a kind of cardboard snobbery which insists that when a man has played four years of football on the college level he either has it or he doesn't and there is no time to waste with him because pro football has to be a game for brain surgeons and advanced atomic researchers.

"I think a lot of us miss it there," says a man who has competed with Lombardi for a great many ballplayers. "He hasn't revolutionized this game. I think Paul Brown was the last man to do that by making us pay attention to detail. But he has out-taught us. After all, he taught school, you know. He simply won by being a better teacher. Some people try to compare him with Tom Landry because both of them were once assistant coaches with the Giants. Well, Landry is more like the brilliant lawyer who writes the brief for the case. Vincent is the man who can take it into court and make it stand up."

So he will be remembered like this. They will remember the tight, closeup pictures of his face with the grin that sometimes looks more like acute acid indigestion than a smile. It should look that way. He gave his front teeth to football as a guard at Fordham.

They will remember him as a man who drove employees beyond the reasonable bounds of physical and mental endurance. But they did, indeed, transcend those bounds and live to make an extra bank deposit each December.

They will remember him for allegiance to the team which he commanded, a sophomoric dream in a professional world but on which he made stand up as no other professional team in the history of sports did.

They will remember him for his uncanny ability to gauge the mood of his players, to know just how far he could push them before he had to back off and give them room to breathe. To motivate the same group of men week after week, year after year, to bring them to a fever pitch at the precise moment you want, requires the delicate touch of a master psychologist. Vince Lombardi manipulated psyches the way a puppet master manipulates his dolls.

They will remember him for his negligence, for Lombardi had a fine mind which, characteristically, he developed to the fullest. "He was as good in the classroom as he was an athlete," says Leo Pacquin, one of the Seven Blocks of Granite at Fordham. "He was just as interested in his report card as he was in the Pitt game."

They will remember him for his peculiar — at times infuriating — lack of communication in many areas with the newspaper reporters and the television people, which perhaps is his greatest paradox because communication is actually his strong point. The strong point of any great teacher.

Finally, because the other side gets told so often, once in awhile it wouldn't be wrong to remember him like this: Once there was a linebacker named Nelson Toburen out of the University of Wichita. He was 24 years old and in a game at Green Bay, he caught Johnny

Unitas slipping out of the pocket and dumped him. John Unitas got up. Nelson Toburen did not.

"I remember," Henry Jordan says, "that he was laying there and the doctor had him and they had to take him to the hospital because his neck was broken. Dr. Nellen held his head all the way in the ambulance and it saved his life. He never played another game of football. I also know that Coach Lombardi paid his salary that year and at least the year after."

Maybe, just maybe, this too had something to do with making Vincent Lombardi a winner.

Afterword
by Vince Lombardi

I owe almost everything to football, in which I have spent the greater part of my life. And I have never lost my respect, my admiration or my love for what I consider a great game.

For over thirty years I have been coaching football — in high school, in the college area and at the professional level. Yet I've never had the time, in all those years, to put together my thoughts on the game and what I consider to be the fundamentals.

To me football is more than diagrams and techniques. It is a lot like life in demanding a man's personal commitment to excellence and to victory. But to achieve success, whatever the job we have, we must pay a price for success. It's like anything worthwhile. It has a price. You have to pay the price to win and you have to pay the price to get to the point where success is possible. Most important, you must pay the price to stay there. Success is not a "sometimes" thing. In other words, you don't do what is right once in a while, but all the time. Success is a habit. Winning is a habit.

Unfortunately, so is losing.

We have all watched people and teams achieve success — a promotion or championship — and then be unable to repeat the next year. Winning the first time is a lot easier than repeating as champions. To succeed again requires dedication, perseverance and, above all, discipline and mental toughness. Truly, I have never known a really successful man who deep in his heart did not understand the grind, the discipline that it takes to win.

Through the years, for better or worse, I've picked up a reputation for being tough. I must admit I have mixed emotions about that. I guess what it comes down to is that success demands singleness of purpose and I demanded "mental toughness" from all my players. There has been a lot written about the mental toughness I have supposedly instilled in my teams. I guess the best way to explain it is that once you have established the goals you want and the price you're willing to pay for success, you can ignore the minor hurts, the opponents' pressure and the temporary failures.

I remember the opening day of practice in Green Bay when I was a head coach for the first time in pro football. Afterward, when I walked back into a locker room, I wanted to cry. The lackadaisical, almost passive attitude was like an insidious disease that had infected the whole squad.

The next day there were almost twenty players in the trainer's room waiting for diathermy or the whirlpool or a rubdown. I blew my stack.

"What is this?" I yelled, "an emergency casualty ward? Get this straight! When you're hurt, you have every right to be here. But this is disgraceful. I have no patience with the small hurts that are bothering most of you. You're going to have to live with small hurts, play with small hurts, if you're going to play for me."

The next day when I walked into that room there were only two players there. So maybe that's how you start building mental toughness. And later on, as our success continued, our mental toughness kept us going in games that looked impossible to win. And the many hurts now seem a small price to have paid for winning.

Football is a game of many lessons in courage, stamina and teamwork. It's a spartan game and requires spartan qualities. Sacrifice, self-discipline, dedication — these are spartan qualities.

There are other lessons in football that apply to life. For example, in the early stages it requires exhausting hard work, to the point of drudgery.

It's a game in which hundreds of thousands of Americans take part, and yet it is completely uninhibited by racial or social barriers.

It is a game of strategy and quick decisions.

Winning requires the right psychological and emotional attitudes.

The only true satisfaction a player receives is the satisfaction that comes from being part of a successful team, regardless of what his own personal ends are. More important, each man contributes to the spirit of the whole, and this spirit is the cohesive force which binds forty talented men into an indomitable team.

I have been quoted as saying, "Winning is the only thing." That's a little out of context. What I said is that "Winning is not everything — but making the effort to win is."

Lately, in our society, it seems that we have sympathy only for the losers and misfits. Let us also cheer for the doers and the winners. The zeal to be first in everything has always been American, to win and to win and to win. Not everyone can be a winner all the time, but everyone can make that effort, that commitment to excellence.

And if we fall a little short of our goals, at least we have the satisfaction of knowing we tried. As President Theodore Roosevelt said: "It is not the critic that counts. . . . The credit belongs to the man who is actually in the arena. . . who strives valiantly, who errs and often comes up short again and again. . . who, at the best, knows in the end the triumph of high achievement, and who at worst, if he fails, at least fails while daring greatly, so that his place shall never be with those cold and timid souls who know neither victory nor defeat."

Each Sunday, after the battle, one group savors victory; another lives in the bitterness of defeat. The practice and the hard work of the season seem a small price for having won. But there are no reasons that are adequate for having lost. For the loser there must be one hundred percent determination and dedication to win next time.

And each day, each week, each year, there is a new encounter, a new challenge. But all of the cheers and all of the color and all of the display linger only in the memory. The spirit, the will to win and the will to excel — these are the things that endure and these are the qualities that are so much more important than any of the events that occasion them.

And I say that the quality of any man's life has got to be a full measure of that man's personal commitment to excellence and to victory, regardless of what field he may be in.

About the Editor

Mike Bynum is one of the South's most successful young authors. He is the author of eight previous books which are all based on football, including the highly successful *Bear Bryant's Boys of Autumn* and *Knute Rockne: His Life and Legend,* and the recently published *Many Autumns Ago: The Frank Leahy Era at Boston College and Notre Dame.* Adding to his list of credits, Mike served as consulting producer to the Mizlou TV special *Bear Bryant — Countdown to 315* which was produced for N.B.C.

A former student manager for Coach Bryant's Crimson Tide football team and honor student at The University of Alabama, Mike is completing a series of biographies on football's greatest coaches. Afterwards, he will be attending law school.